THE IRAN-IRAQ WAR

THE IRAN-IRAQ WAR

An Historical, Economic and Political Analysis

Edited by M.S. El Azhary

ST. MARTIN'S PRESS
New York
and
Centre for Arab Gulf Studies, University of Exeter
Centre for Arab Gulf Studies, University of Basra

© 1984 M. S. El Azhary
All rights reserved. For information, write:
St. Martin's Press, Inc., 175 Fifth Avenue, New York, NY 10010
Printed in Great Britain
First published in the United States of America in 1984

Library of Congress Cataloging in Publication Data
Main entry under title:

The Iran-Iraq War.

   Chiefly papers presented at a symposium entitled
"Shatt al-Arab", held at the University of Exeter in
July 1982.
   Includes index.
   1. Iraqi-Iranian Conflict, 1980–   —Congresses.
2. Near East—Politics and government —1945–   —Congresses.
I. El Azhary, M. S.

DS318.8.I694   1984   955′.054   83-16148
ISBN 0-312-43583-5

CONTENTS

TABLES AND MAPS

Tables

Maps

PREFACE

Most of the articles in this book were originally presented as papers to
to a symposium entitled 'Shatt al-Arab' which was convened at the
University of Exeter in July 1982. The symposium was held under the
joint auspices of the Centre for Arab Gulf Studies, University of Exeter,
and the Centre for Arab Gulf Studies, University of Basra. I would like
to thank the staff of both Centres for their hard work in organizing the
symposium.

Thanks are also due to all those who participated in the symposium,
whose comments have enabled several of the speakers to refine the
arguments presented in the symposium version of their papers. Several
Iranian specialists were invited but disappointingly only two accepted
the invitation and participated, adding to the lively discussions that
characterized the symposium proceedings.

I am grateful to the technicians and cartographers of the Geography
Department, University of Exeter, for the preparation of the maps.

To Mrs Sheila Westcott, who typed the manuscript with expertise
and patience, I extend my appreciation.

M. S. El Azhary

1 INTRODUCTION

M. S. El Azhary

The Iran-Iraq war which broke out in September 1980 and which continues unabated in 1983 has brought death and suffering to hundreds of thousands of people on both sides, and it has devastated the economies of both countries. It has also increased international tension by precipitating new alliances and a rearrangement of forces in the already turbulent Middle East. And although the war, so far, has been limited to the two countries, it still has the potential danger of spreading the fighting at any moment to the rest of the oil-rich Gulf region, with incalculable results both for the states in the area and the world at large.

The focus of this book is on the historical, economic and political dimensions of the war between Iraq and Iran. It examines many aspects of what has proved to be a very complex conflict, including its long history, its present economic and political setting, the different responses to the war by outside parties and its regional and worldwide implications. But before embarking on an analysis of the intricacies of the conflict that are offered in the following articles, an overview of the main developments in the war during the past three years is in order.

In early 1979, after the Shi'a Islamic revolution seized power in Iran, the new regime began exporting its brand of revolution to Iraq through a propaganda campaign aimed mainly at the Shi'a community, which comprises more than half the Iraqi population, inciting it to revolt against the Sunni-dominated Baathist regime. Iranian leaders attacked the ideology of the Baath party as anti-Islamic, and Ayatollah Khomeini repeatedly called for the overthrow of the regime of Saddam Hussein, whom he called an enemy of Islam and Muslims. These and other calls by the Iranian leadership were accompanied by a terror campaign of bombing incidents and assassination attempts on Iraqi officials which were carried out by members of a right-wing Iranian guerrilla group.

The result was an atmosphere of fear and tension in Baghdad. The Iraqi government took the Iranian actions seriously and responded in a way that showed it was willing to go to war to put an end to them. First, Iraq countered with a propaganda campaign of its own. It denounced the 'Persian magicians led by Khomeini' and called for the overthrow of his regime. Radio Baghdad openly indulged in the racial stereotype that the Persians were dangerous and devious people and it appealed to the Arab world's dislike of *al-'ajam* — the non-Arab Muslims of the East.

Secondly, Baghdad armed and trained guerrillas who waged a sabotage campaign against Iranian oil installations. The Iraqi government also took reprisals by expelling tens of thousands of persons of Persian descent from southern Iraq. Thirdly, Iraq opened up its old territorial disputes with Iran which seemed to have been settled in the deal Iraq made with the Shah in 1975. Iraq called for a revision of the agreement on the demarcation of the border along the Shatt al-Arab; for a return to Arab ownership of the three islands in the Strait of Hormuz which the Shah seized in 1971; and, most dangerously of all, for the granting of autonomy to the minorities inside Iran. The granting of this last demand would have led to the fragmentation of the present Iranian empire, and this in turn might have led to a secessionist movement among the Arab community in the oil-rich province of Khuzistan in southern Iran.

In the meantime, sporadic skirmishes along the frontier became serious and more frequent. Throughout 1980 both sides were reporting tank, artillery and aircraft bombardment of their positions. But with Iran in the throes of revolutionary chaos, its armed forces appeared inferior to those of Iraq in material, morale, organization and discipline. So the Iraqi leadership was greatly tempted to grab the oilfields in southern Iran — which they tried to do when full-scale fighting erupted in September of the same year. They hoped that a quick victory on the battlefield, coupled with increasing their support to the anti-Khomeini forces inside Iran, would weaken further the regime in Tehran and thus force the Iranian government to accept Iraqi demands.

With this bold move Iraq was claiming the mantle of the dominant power in the Gulf region, the same role played by Iran under the Shah in the 1970s. But after a few weeks of fighting, the Iraqi armed forces had captured only a few hundred square miles of Iranian territory, which was not a sufficiently clear victory to bring about such grandiose results. The war soon developed into a stalemate, with the Iraqis prevented from advancing further or consolidating their hold on the occupied areas. This situation continued for months on end with no significant military action by either side.

To be sure, there was considerable damage done in these first few weeks of the war to the major towns in southern Iran, and to the oil installations of both sides. Iraq's oil exports from Khor al-Amaya and Mina al-Bakr at the head of the Gulf ceased because the loading terminals were badly damaged and the Syrians had closed one of the pipelines to the Mediterranean, thus limiting Iraq to the use of only one pipeline via Turkey. The Iranians, on the other hand, were able to restore their oil exports from Kharg island and the other terminals further down the Gulf. It is important to note, however, that after this initial damage to the oil installations of both countries, the two sides abided by an unwritten understanding that neither side would inflict further damage on the other's oil installations. Under these circumstances Iran has been able to pay for its own war effort, while Iraq has had to depend on Arab financial aid that has diminished in recent months.

In the spring of 1982 the Iranian armed forces regrouped and were able to dislodge and push back the Iraqis across the border. Now it was the turn of the Iranian leadership to try to implement a grandiose scheme of its own with the overall aim of regaining the dominant regional role Iran once had. In the following July Khomeini unleashed his army along the Shatt al-Arab in a huge invasion of Iraq. His objective was not just the overthrow of Saddam Hussein, but the creation of an Iraqi Islamic republic modelled on that of Iran. Khomeini now was insisting that reparations for the damage from the war must come from Iraq. But the Iranian invasion failed, with the Iraqi armed forces performing better in defence of their homeland. Since then they have also succeeded in repulsing several other major Iranian offensives.

Soon the war reverted to a stalemate; it did not trigger a Shi'a rebellion in southern Iraq, just as the earlier invasion of Khuzistan had failed to produce a liberation movement there. In fact, the war seems to have had the opposite effect: it has had the unintended result of increasing national pride and support for both regimes among their respective populations. Death and destruction, however, have been extensive, with the number of dead and casualties estimated in the hundreds of thousands. In economic terms, the devastation is incalculable on both sides: losses are estimated in tens of billions of dollars from the loss of oil revenues and the destruction of oil and other installations.

At the regional level, the war has not so far spilled into neighbouring states, nor has it obstructed access to oil from the Gulf; both parties have adhered to their declared desire of keeping the Strait of Hormuz open to shipping. Moreover, the United States has dispatched the AWACS (Airborne Warning and Control System) reconnaissance planes to Saudi Arabia to deter Iran from widening the war. In this respect, Iraq has been viewed as the less dangerous of the two combatants, considering its improved relations in recent years with Saudi Arabia, the smaller Gulf States, Jordan and Egypt, all of which have sided with Iraq in the war and given it financial as well as logistical support. Iraq has also improved its relations with the West generally, and increased her arms purchases from France.

Furthermore, Iraq has split from the Steadfastness and Confrontation Front, whose members — Syria, Libya, South Yemen (PDRY) and Algeria — have sided with Iran in the war; thus a new divisive factor has been introduced into inter-Arab politics. Consequently, this division in Arab ranks has produced the negative effect of shifting Arab concerns away from the Arab-Israeli conflict; it also encouraged the Reagan administration to neglect this problem and feel no urgency to reactivate the search for peace until disaster struck in Lebanon in the summer of 1982. From Lebanese and Palestinian perspectives, it was this distraction and neglect that gave Israel a free hand on such an unprecedented scale, bringing calamitous results for both peoples.

The two superpowers have found it advantageous to stay neutral towards the war between Iraq and Iran. Although their stakes in the conflict remain high, both lack leverage to influence the course of the conflict. Yet both have expressed concern, because it is in their interest to avoid the danger of the fragmentation or dismemberment of either side.

The articles in this book cover four broad aspects of the Shatt al-Arab dispute, each of which contributes to an overall understanding of the present conflict. First, in a historical survey of the long antagonism between the two sides and the strategic importance of the Shatt al-Arab for them both, Peter Hünseler (Chapter 2: The Historical Antecedents of the Shatt al-Arab Dispute) shows that for centuries both countries have made claims and counterclaims on each other's territory, supporting their respective positions by ethnic, political or religious arguments. Mustafa al-Najjar and Najdat Fathi Safwat (Chapter 3: Arab Sovereignty over the Shatt al-Arab during the Ka'bide Period) chronicle the history of the Arab dynasty of the Bani Ka'b, who in the seventeenth and eighteenth centuries established their domain east of the Shatt al-Arab in Arabistan and imposed Arab sovereignty over the Shatt.

Second, the economic and political setting of the present conflict is examined in three articles. David Long (Chapter 4: Oil and the Iran-Iraq War) shows how the shift to alternative sources of energy, in progress since the 1973–4 oil price rise, combined with market forces to moderate the impact of the war on the worldwide demand for oil. Long assesses the devastating impact of the war on the Iraqi and Iranian oil sectors. John Townsend (Chapter 5: Economic and Political Implications of the War: the Economic Consequences for the Participants) looks at the effects of the war on the major economic activities of both countries, particularly foreign trade, economic development programmes and manpower. Basil al-Bustany (Chapter 6: Development Strategy in Iraq and the War Effort: the Dynamics of Challenge) focuses mainly on the impact of the war on the five-year plan of 1981–5; he goes into greater detail about how the development programmes are being implemented so far. Although al-Bustany's assessment is written from a different perspective than that of Townsend, the two are not necessarily incompatible.

Third, in the international field, the external attitudes to the Iran-Iraq war and its regional and worldwide implications are examined in three articles. G. H. Jansen (Chapter 7: The Attitudes of the Arab Governments towards the Gulf War) explains the varied reasons behind the lack of support for Iraq from most Arab states. M. S. El Azhary (Chapter 8: The Attitudes of the Superpowers towards the Gulf War) analyses the positions taken by both superpowers towards the conflict in the context of their bilateral relations with both Iraq and Iran. From a different perspective, and with a wider scope than in the two previous articles, John Duke Anthony (Chapter 9: Regional and Worldwide Implications of the Gulf War) evaluates the concerns of the outside world at the regional and global levels.

Fourth, the prospects for a peaceful settlement of the Gulf war are assessed in the final article by Glen Balfour-Paul (Chapter 10: The Prospects for Peace) in the light of his analysis of the real issues in dispute between the two combatants. This also sheds some light on the failure of all the attempts at mediation made so far in this conflict.

Map 1.1: International Boundary Line Between Iraq and Iran

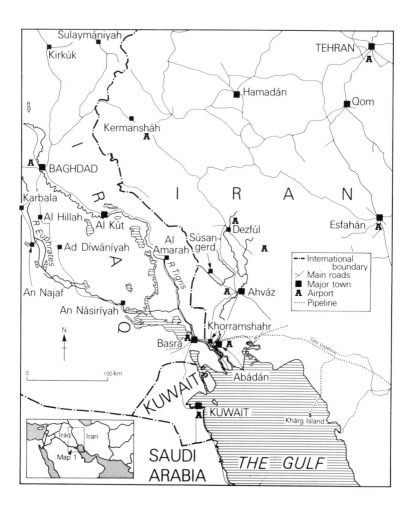

Map 1.2: The Shatt al-Arab Frontier, Algiers Agreement (6 March 1975)

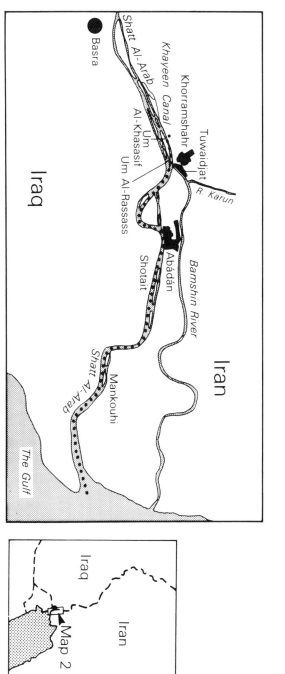

2 THE HISTORICAL ANTECEDENTS OF THE SHATT AL-ARAB DISPUTE

Peter Hünseler

The Shatt al-Arab Dispute in the Overall Context of Persian-Arab Antagonism

Unlike the course taken by other peoples who came under subjection in the Arab conquests of the seventh century, Persia succeeded in maintaining its national character against the invaders. When, in AD 636, the Persian Sassanids were defeated at the Battle of Qadisiya near Hira by the Arab armies of General Sa'd bin Abi Waqqas and the empire itself came to an end with the Battle of Nihawand in 642, its population, conscious of the state's territorial integrity and cultural continuity, converted to Islam. The conquering Arabs and the peoples they subjected considered Arabism and Islam a unity; the Persian culture, however, 'though overlaid by Islam, could not be suppressed'.[1]

A key principle which has permeated Persian history since the Arab conquests, and strongly influenced its current social and political life, is that of a juxtaposition of Persia and Islam. This principle has arisen out of the Zoroastrian view of a state which tends towards a secularly-legitimized kingship, the survival of the Persian language (albeit soon written in Arabic script) and the proud awareness of a distinct Persian history. Within only two centuries, the Sunni-Arab caliphate of the Abbasids had come to find Persian literature attractive. Real power was seized, time and again, by the Persian dynasties in the Abbasid caliphate. Between 954 and 1055 — for over a century — the Buyid dynasty managed to control political events in Iraq and western Persia and to restrict the Abbasid caliphs to a purely religious role. 'Thus the history of the Buyids in Iraq can bee understood as a struggle between Arabism and Persianism'.[2]

The adoption of Shi'ism as the state religion in Persia by the Safavids early in the sixteenth century constituted the zenith of Persia's delimitation from its Arab neighbours, while remaining within the context of Islam. For the first time in the history of

8

Islam, Shi'ism thereby established itself in a state, thus fragmenting, in a way previously unknown, the unity of the Islamic world. The Safavid kings viewed themselves primarily as secular rulers and left religious leadership to the theologians. The Shi'a clergy subsequently became unwilling to relinquish the powerful position they had acquired under the Safavids. Especially under the early Qajar rulers, land and money had been lavished upon them, gaining for their leaders economic independence from the monarchy and a steady growth of influence in Persian politics. No comparable development had taken place in the neighbouring Sunni Arab states.

A new dimension had therefore been added to the original contradiction between Arab and Persian nationalism: the Sunni-Shi'a antagonism. In that context, adherence to divergent branches of Islam proved less significant than the differing degree of influence exerted by religion on the formation and appreciation of politics and state power. That condition still prevails today, particularly in those states in which an *Arab* population is divided into Sunnis and Shi'a.

The leaders of the Shi'a clergy in the Arab states (Iraq, Bahrain) could not attain an exclusive social position comparable to that in Persia, where the Shi'a acquired a national religious importance. Hence these Shi'a clerics found themselves exposed to a dual conflict of loyalty: on the one hand, they preached Shi'ism in a state not homogenously Shi'a and were thus drawn into the historic antagonism between Sunni and Shi'a; on the other, as *Arab* Shi'a they were suspected by their Arab rulers of succumbing to non-Arab (in other words, Persian) influence. Only too often they were perceived by their Arab compatriots as representing foreign, non-Arab interests. The Arab Shi'a's perennial dissociation from their political leaders evidently originates here, apart from their mistrust of any secular rule, a mistrust grounded in Shi'a chiliasm.

Persian-Arab antagonism and the struggle for influence and predominance in the Middle East naturally manifested itself chiefly where Sunni and Shi'a population groups, as well as Arabs and Persians, clashed in their settlement areas. While Persians and the Arabs of the Arabian peninsula were separated geographically by the Persian-Arab Gulf, antagonism appeared clearly along the land boundaries. The determination of a common border thus became a conflict lasting several centuries, in the course of which each side repeatedly claimed vast territories of the other state. These claims were corroborated historically, ethnically, geopolitically or by way of religious arguments. The economic and strategic significance of the Shatt al-Arab for both sides gave the border definition in this area an importance well beyond that of all other controversies.

The war that broke out in September 1980 between Iran and Iraq is a further element in the lengthy struggle by both sides for delimitation, influence, and predominance in the region. Contrary to earlier conflicts, however, in which both sides were forced into a compromise by major European powers according to their own interests in the region, Iran and Iraq went to war in 1980 with the uncompromising goal of achieving only their own respective claims. They employed all the strategies which have marked the long history of the conflict: intervention in each other's internal affairs, mutual territorial claims (Iran to the Shatt al-Arab and Bahrain; Iraq to the Shatt and Arabistan/Khuzistan), and different idelogical orientations.

The Shatt al-Arab Dispute between Persia and the Ottoman Empire

The Peace Treaty of 1639

After the conquest of Baghdad in 1638 by the Turkish Sultan Murad IV, the first border settlement with Persia was arrived at as early as the following year. Since both in the north (Kurds, Armenians) and in the south (Arabs) the boundary cut through traditional settlement areas of tribes which 'regarded as their natural masters'[3] neither the Turks nor the Persians, the course of the border was not laid down exactly or in any detail, but conformed, for the most part, to tribal loyalties and toponyms. This accommodated the wishes of both sides to make further territorial gains by closely linking the tribes to either Esfahan or Istanbul. Although frequent boundary disputes flared up thereafter, in the Kurdish-Armenian boundary district, they could be settled on the basis of the 1639 agreement. For the boundary course in the Shatt al-Arab region, however, this agreement proved insufficient. From the Persian point of view, the Shatt al-Arab constituted a natural border; the Turkish perspective, however, was that the Arab tribes on both sides of the Shatt al-Arab constituted an ethnic and historical unit, from which they concluded that Arabistan, including the Shatt al-Arab, belonged to the Ottoman Empire.

The Second Erzerum Treaty of 1847

When, in 1823, new boundary disputes erupted around Muhammarah and the Persians occupied that city, Great Britain and Russia offered their good offices. On 15 May 1843 a Turkish-Persian-British-Russian boundary commission met in the Turkish city of Erzerum to try to reach a final border settlement based on the Agreement of 1639. On 31 May 1847, after four years of tough negotiations, the parties settled on a treaty containing essentially the following points:[4]

(1) The city and harbour anchorage of Muhammarah and the island of Khidhr (now Abadan) were ceded to Persia; in return, Turkey received territorial concessions in the provinces of Zuhab and Sulaymaniyah (Article 2).

(2) A boundary commission was appointed *in situ* to mark the precise course of the boundary in mutual agreement (Article 3).

(3) The Ottoman Empire was awarded the Shatt al-Arab in its entire breadth up to the deep-water marker on the eastern shore, save for the above-mentioned territories of Muhammarah and the island of Khidhr.

The treaty of 1847 suffered from a central weakness: it remained largely nebulous in its wording and was unclear about the course of the border in the Shatt al-Arab region, thus leaving unresolved the question of territorial responsibility for the eastern bank of the river. Even though the Shatt al-Arab remained under Turkish sovereignty in its total width, the course of the border was not specified *expressis verbis*.

Because the Turkish government insisted on a clarification of the treaty's imprecise handling of the affiliation of Arabistan/Khuzistan, the signatory powers, Great Britain and Russia, declared in an 'explanatory note' that this question had not been prejudiced by the wording of the treaty. Turkey bluntly refused to ratify the treaty unless Persia recognized the 'explanatory note' as 'part and parcel' of the treaty. The Persian representative, Mirza Muhammad Ali Khan, also signed this 'explantory note', unknown to the Persian government. When the Persian government learned of the existence of this additional note, it declared its approval null and void on the grounds that the Persian delegate had not been authorized to sign.

Despite these differences, the boundary commission, appointed in accordance with Article 3, visited the Turkish-Persian border in the years 1850–2. The commission's work, however, was hampered considerably by the divergent conceptions of the Turkish and Persian commissioners. The Persian side took the position that the treaty had granted Persia the entire territory east of the Shatt al-Arab, whereas the Turkish side referred to the 'explanatory note' as leaving this question open. As no resolution was possible, given these existing differences, the commission continued its work north of the Shatt al-Arab so that the boundary delimitation in the Shatt al-Arab region itself was dropped for the time being.

The Constantinople Protocol of 1913

In the following years Persia made various appeals to Britain and Russia to resume their mediation in the border question. Persia's goal was to assume, with Turkey, joint control of the Shatt al-Arab, in addition to the harbour and anchoring rights laid down in the treaty. The policies of Britain and Russia had been at cross-purposes since the mid-nineteenth century, however, thereby exacerbating Anglo-Russian tensions. Their readiness, therefore, to mediate in the Shatt al-Arab conflict was considerably reduced. It was only after the signing of the Anglo-Russian convention of 31 August 1907, after which Persia was divided into three zones — a Russian sphere of influence in the north, a British sphere in the south, and a neutral zone in the middle — that Anglo-Russian interest in a clearly defined Persian-Turkish border was reawakened.

Russia's interests centred on the Persian province of Azerbaijan, due to economic and strategic considerations relating to Turkey. Britain's position on the boundary question differed from that of Russia, in that British interests were not restricted to Persia (the discovery of oil deposits, and so on). They included the Turkish side of the Shatt al-Arab, which played a considerable part in the wider context of British policy towards the Gulf. In July 1911 Anglo-Turkish negotiations towards a comprehensive agreement clarifying the rights and claims of both sides in the Persian-Arab Gulf area got underway. The agreement was eventually signed by Britain and Turkey on 29 July 1913. It contained, aside from a settlement of the status of several Arab shaikhdoms, a series of further agreements relating to the Shatt al-Arab which became important owing to growing British influence in Iraq and

Arabistan. By means of these agreements, Britain advanced to the role of the Shatt al-Arab's hegemonic power, next to Turkey, and thus a clear adjustment of the border along the Shatt to Turkey's advantage was in Britain's interest. Russia, which, as 'arbitrating power' with Britain, had participated in determining the Turkish-Persian border and also pursued maritime interests in the Shatt and the Gulf, was surprised by Britain's unilateral action and rejected the Anglo-Turkish agreement. Russian interests were affected in particular by Britain's relinquishing the entire Shatt al-Arab to Turkey. But in view of Britain's assurance that it would support Russian interests in the northern part of the Turkish-Persian border, Russia reconsidered its earlier decision and accepted the Anglo-Turkish arrangements. Thus the way was clear for the opening of new negotiations among the four powers.

Meanwhile, in the protocol of 21 December 1911, the Persian Foreign Minister and the Turkish envoy in Tehran had agreed to appoint a Turkish-Persian boundary commission in Istanbul to reach an accord on the basis of the Second Treaty of Erzerum. The commission started work in March 1912 and by August of that year had met 18 times. At first, success seemed to be precluded, given Persia's persistent refusal to recognize the 'note explicative' of 26 April 1847. However, due to Russian pressure, Tehran finally accepted the 'explanatory note' at the second-to-last session (15 August 1912). The preliminary work of the Turkish-Persian commission was complemented by a series of notes and declarations which found expression in the Four-Power Protocol of Constantinople on 17 November 1913. In the Shatt al-Arab region, the course of the border was setttled in accordance with the Second Treaty of Erzerum of 1847, i.e. the Shatt remained Turkish waters for its entire expanse except for the restrictions at Muhammarah and Abadan. Pursuant to the Four-Power Agreement of November 1913, two-thirds of the total border had been settled in detail. The fixing of the entire boundary was assigned to a Four-Power Delimitation Commission which was to mark the border on location, based on the 'carte identique' of 1869. Early in 1914 the border delimitation commission began its work. The outbreak of the First World War, however, prevented recognition of the border by Turkey and Persia.

The Shatt al-Arab Dispute between Iran and Iraq

The Treaty of 1937

The aftermath of the First World War produced completely novel conditions for the border question along the Shatt al-Arab. Quite naturally, the British mandate of Iraq, which had come about in Mesopotamia, entered into the Turkish boundary claims against Iran, although it also impinged upon British navigational privileges on the Shatt al-Arab which had gained significance.

Meanwhile Iran had also undergone a major political change. With Muhammad Reza Khan's assumption of power in 1921, it became increasingly evident that Iran was unwilling to accept the contractual agreements on the Shatt al-Arab. The defeat, also in 1921, of the anglophile Shaikh of Muhammarah, Khaz'al, permitted Iran to protect its interests even more strongly along the Shatt al-Arab. The strengthening of Iranian claims in Arabistan meant that Britain must henceforth enforce its rights without endangering its interests in Iran.

Due to Iraqi claims to jurisdiction over the Shatt al-Arab, Iran at first refused to accord diplomatic recognition to Iraq. However, in 1929 Iran recognized Iraq, in the hope that Britain, as the mandatary power in Iraq, would take Iranian wishes into account. Britain, given its economic involvement in Iran (in the Anglo-Persian Oil Company), was directly interested in the Shatt al-Arab question, and especially in unimpeded access to the refineries at Abadan. Through an exchange of identical notes by the Iraqi and Iranian governments (11 August 1929) a *modus vivendi* was found to regulate relations between the two countries, pending the conclusion of detailed agreements on friendship and trade, as well as an agreement on navigation. However, the Shatt al-Arab negotiations foundered on the non-acceptance, by Iraq and Britain, of Iranian sovereignty over the 'Iranian half' of the river.

When Britain prepared to end its mandate in Iraq and concluded an alliance with Iraq in 1930, it explicitly reserved the right of the British navy to enter the Shatt al-Arab at any time, even in peacetime. Nevertheless, it became increasingly obvious that the Iranian government was not interested in amicable bilateral agreement, nor did it recognize the border as valid. On 25 March 1924 the Iranian government had declared that it did not recognize the boundary settlement of the Constantinople Protocol; and further identical declarations were made on 20 September and 2 December 1931.

The conflict escalated when, on 9 November 1932, Iran ordered four gunboats into the Shatt al-Arab as far as Muhammarah. The conflict added fuel to the pilot issue and the problem of the ships' flags.

The accumulating boundary clashes (also along the border north of the Shatt al-Arab) and the almost daily conflicts resulting from the unsolved flag and pilot questions prompted the Iranian government to turn to the League of Nations on 29 November 1934, but neither the League of Nations nor the rapporteurs dispatched by it succeeded in bridging the differences. Only the planned Middle East pact initiated in 1935 by Iran with Turkish assistance, which was also supported by Iraq, prepared the terrain for bilateral talks and a contractual settlement of all the points at issue. On 4 July 1937 an Iranian-Iraqi border treaty was signed in Tehran which, on the whole, confirmed the Protocols of Constantinople of 1913/14. Accordingly, the Iran-Iraq border continued to run along the east bank of the Shatt al-Arab; beside the special arrangements concerning Muhammarah and Abadan, Iran was now granted a four-mile anchorage zone off Abadan (Article 2). Furthermore it was agreed to open the Shatt al-Arab to merchantmen of all nations and naval vessels of the two contracting parties. The transit fees were to be used for the maintenance and expansion of the shipping lanes in the Shatt al-Arab. Even though the river was assigned to Iraqi jurisdiction in its whole breadth, this was not to infringe upon the user rights of either nation (Article 4). All other technical questions relating to shipping in the Shatt al-Arab were left for a convention to be worked out jointly (Article 5). In an additional protocol, both sides undertook to adopt this convention within two years subsequent to the agreement's conclusion. This, however, did not come to pass. On 8 December 1938 an Iranian-Iraqi boundary commission started work at the confluence of the Khayeen and the Shatt al-Arab, but again the commission's work was frustrated by differing interpretations of the treaty and the final delimitation of the border on location. The joint convention on technical shipping questions stipulated by Article 5 of the treaty fared similarly. The Iranian agreement aimed its proposals at equal control and protection of the shipping lanes in the Shatt. The Iraqi government viewed this as an attempt by Iran to use the convention to undermine Iraqi sovereign rights on the Shatt.

The Shatt al-Arab Dispute in the 1950s

The political constellation of the year 1955 and the founding of the Baghdad Pact again produced advantageous conditions for both sides to settle their differences contractually. On the occasion of a state visit to Iran by Iraq's King Faisal in October 1957 both sides agreed to settle their differences based on the following points:

(1) The appointment of a mixed commission to work out a convention on the joint administration of the Shatt al-Arab with its seat in Baghdad.

(2) The transfer of the border-marking to a Swedish arbitrator, based in Tehran, with the participation of an Iraqi-Iranian commission.

The hopes for an Iranian-Iraqi agreement were dashed by the outbreak of the revolution in Baghdad on 14 July 1958.

The change of regime in Baghdad soon caused a renewed deterioration of the Iranian-Iraqi relationship and a revival of the border disputes along the Shatt al-Arab and in the area of the land boundary. Only four months after General Abd al-Karim Qasim seized power, the Iraqi revolutionary government announced a unilateral expansion of its coastal waters to 12 miles. One year later, in a press conference on 28 November 1959, Shah Reza Pahlevi renewed the demand for the border line to run along the centre of the Shatt al-Arab because Iraq was not obeying the stipulations of the treaty of 1937. He justified his demand by arguing that, in the twentieth century, a boundary river could no longer belong to the exclusive jurisdiction of either riparian. Qasim replied to the Iranian demand with his own claim for the return of the four-mile anchorage zone off Abadan granted to Iran in the treaty of 1937. At the same time Qasim advocated a peaceful solution of the dispute. The hint at a peaceful solution of the problems obviously represented a sign by Baghdad, directed towards Tehran, that the Iraqi demand for the four-mile anchorage zone would be dropped if Tehran definitively recognized Iraq's claims along the Shatt al-Arab and hence the treaty of 1937. This, however, was rejected by Iran's Foreign Minister, Abbas Aram, on 10 December 1959. On 19 December General Qasim once again commented on Iraq's legal claims to the four-mile zone without mentioning the demand for its return. He concluded his statement with an unmistakable hint at the Arab territories of Muhammarah and

Ahvaz, which had been an integral part of Iraq prior to their secession to the Ottoman Empire. Simultaneously he diffused his remarks on Arabistan with a call to Iran to honour existing treaties. He recommended a solution in the context of the United Nations. A renewed escalation occurred when the Iranian newspaper *Ettelaat* maintained, on 19 December, that 'the existence of Iraq was in any event a historical misunderstanding and the whole of Iraq a Persian province'.

Although there were short-term troop concentrations on the Iranian side, an outbreak of armed clashes could have been avoided. The clashes were due less to a mutual lack of will to normalize their goals and claims, militarily if necessary, than to concrete foreign political threats to which both sides felt themselves exposed. After the conclusion of the defence agreement with the United States on 5 March 1959, Iran found itself increasingly pressured by Moscow and therefore feared the growing Soviet influence in revolutionary Iraq for two reasons: on the one hand, it felt exposed to the danger of a Soviet pincer; on the other hand, Iran feared a spread of revolutionary ideas to the Iranian opposition. Iraq, for its part, felt threatened on its western flank by the United Arab Republic, created in 1958 through the fusion of Egypt and Syria. Abd al-Karim Qasim feared massive support for Iraqi Nasserites from neighbouring Syria in the event of a military dispute with Iran. Thus the 'war' was waged only by the mass media on both sides and soon dissolved. For the first time, however, the dispute reflected the ideological antagonism of both states. Aside from differing views of the legal questions, opposing positions on the social order now appeared for the first time, which in the following years added a regional dimension to the conflict.

The Algiers Agreement of March 1975

When in 1967 British Prime Minister Harold Wilson announced his government's intention to withdraw British military units 'east of Suez', Iran prepared to maintain the existing power relations through its own forced rearmament so as to assume Britain's role on the day of the British withdrawal. The closing of the Suez Canal in 1967 was a positive factor as it impeded operations of the Soviet navy in the region. In security matters, Iran sought the collaboration of the conservative Arab Gulf states under the leadership of Tehran, to be directed primarily against the influence of the Soviet Union as well as at revolutionary movements and states (Iraq,

South Yemen). The Arab Gulf States adopted a temporizing policy towards the Iranian courting: on the one hand, they could scarcely enter into an open alliance with an Iran that was supportive of Israel; on the other hand, they wanted to avoid an open split of the Arab Gulf riparians.

Iran redoubled its efforts to become the hegemonic power in the Persian-Arab Gulf and, in 1969, denounced the Iraqi-Iranian treaty of 1937. In order to dominate and control the shipping lanes in the Gulf, it seemed imperative to the Shah that the Iranian navy be able to operate unhindered in the Shatt al-Arab, the more so since this would deliver the two most important Iranian ports on the Shatt, Khorramshahr and Abadan, from Iraqi control. To establish free Iranian navigation on the Shatt, an Iranian ship, unannounced and without an Iraqi navigation pilot, left the port of Khorramshahr under the protection of Iranian patrol boats and reached the Persian-Arab Gulf without incident. Although Iraq was not ready to accept this breach of contractual agreements without protest, it was markedly inferior to Iran militarily in 1969. Moreover, Iraq found itself, one year after the assumption of power by the Baath party, in a phase of internal power consolidation which tied its forces domestically.

This policy of weakening Iraq internally was consistently pursued by the Shah, especially after 1972. Upon the conclusion of the Iraqi-Soviet friendship treaty of 1972, the Shah arranged with American President Richard Nixon for massive support of the Kurds in Iraq so as to neutralize the Iraqi army regionally through domestic action. Thus, in August 1972, new unrest broke out in Kurdistan. The Iraqi government and the Kurdish leader Mullah Mustafa Barzani had worked out an autonomy statute for Kurdistan in March 1970, which was to be implemented in 1974 after a four-year transitional period. This peaceful settlement of the Kurdish question in Iraq was seriously imperilled by the Iranian-American support for Barzani. In effect, Kurdish fighters refused to relinquish their weapons and end the civil war in March 1974 at the conclusion of the transitional phase. The Iraqi army, increasingly equipped with Russian weapons in the wake of the Iraqi-Soviet friendship treaty, was soon able to achieve military successes in Kurdistan. After the rapid fall of the cities of Zakhu and Rowanduz, the Iraqi army succeeded in herding the Kurdish resistance fighters into a small area near the Iranian border. Crucial defects in the army's ammunition, and the Soviet refusal to supply more arms, threatened to undo its successes against the Kurds. In early March 1975 the Iraqi leadership therefore accepted an offer by Iran to desist from supporting the Kurds, provided Iraq agreed to a border settlement with Iran to establish the course of the border in the Shatt al-Arab region along the *thalweg* line.

On 13 June 1975 Iran and Iraq signed a treaty in Baghdad containing, in essence, four points:

(1) The definitive marking of the boundaries, in accordance with the Constantinople Protocol of 1913 and the proposal submitted by the committee for boundary markings of 1914.
(2) The establishment of the river boundaries along the *thalweg* line, i.e. in mid-river.
(3) The re-establishment of security along the shared land boundaries, and of mutual trust, and an end to infiltrations of a subversive nature on both sides.
(4) The recognition of all points as unrenounceable conditions of a general settlement of the problem.

By signing the treaty on 13 June 1975, Iraq recognized for the first time the *thalweg* principle for the Shatt al-Arab. But five years later it became clear that it had agreed only under considerable pressure from Iran, and through the fact that the Soviet Union had refused to deliver the missing ammunition. Nevertheless, the concessions in the Shatt al-Arab question opened the way for an ending of the civil war in Kurdistan.

In August 1978, however, the strategic importance of the Shatt al-Arab for Iran was considerably reduced, because Iran moved its naval forces from Khorramshahr to the Gulf port of Bandar Abbas.

Notes

2. Heribert Busse, *Das kulturelle Erbe Persiens und der Islam* (The Cultural Heritage of Persia and Islam) (Bonn, 1979), p. 1.

2. Heribert Busse, *Chalif und Groskonig: Die Buyiden im Iraq* (Caliph and King: The Buyids in Iraq) (Steiner, Wiesbaden, 1969), p. 8.

3. Ulrich Gehrke and Gustave Kuhn, *Die Grenzen des Irak. Historische und rechtliche Aspekte des irakischen Anspruchs auf Kuwait und des irakischpersischen Streits um den Schatt al-Arab* (The Boundaries of Iraq. Historical and Legal Aspects of the Iraqi Claim on Kuwait and the Iraqi-Iranian Dispute on the Shatt al-Arab) (Kohlhammer, Stuttgart, 1963), p. 176.

3 ARAB SOVEREIGNTY OVER THE SHATT AL-ARAB DURING THE KA'BIDE PERIOD

Mustafa al-Najjar and Najdat Fathi Safwat

The eastern bank of the Shatt al-Arab has been a purely Arab area since ancient times. The population has been overwhelmingly Arab, and its language Arabic. It has been ruled by successive Arab dynasties, such as the Musha'sha'aides, the Bani Ka'b, and finally the Emirates of Muhammarah which were overthrown by Rieza Shah in 1925. Until 1925, 99 per cent of the population was Arab. This percentage, however, has changed as a result of immigration, mass resettlement and the policy of 'Persianization' imposed on the area.

The Arab character of the area led to its being called Arabistan — a name given it by the Persians themselves, and by which it has always been known and described. It was only changed to Khuzistan as recently as 1925, but the new name was restricted to official usage, while Arabistan remained in everyday use by the people of the area and elsewhere in Iran.

This article deals with one of the most important periods in the history of the Arabian Gulf — the emergence and rise of the Bani Ka'b (the Ka'bide dynasty) in the mid-seventeenth century as a new power on the east and west of the Shatt al-Arab. This Arab power was able to play an active role in the life of the area, imposing sovereignty over its lands, and deterring attempts by other powers to intrude upon its sphere of influence and jeopardize its rights.[1]

The clans of the Bani Ka'b tribe came from Iraq in search of security and independence.[2] Longrigg relates that they were a rice-growing, stock-breeding Arab tribe from Lower Arabistan,[3] who contributed to the development of the economic life and prosperity of the area.

The Bani Ka'b were assisted by the neighbouring Musha'sha'aide Emirate (Howaiza), whose Emir had pledged his loyalty to the Ottoman Sultan Sulayman (the Magnificent) during his conquest of Iraq a century earlier,[4] a gesture that confirmed him in his position. The Emir, however, was wavering in his loyalty between the Ottomans and the Persians,[5] maintaining the independence of his

20

principality by playing off one side against the other. Such was his control over the Shatt al-Arab that no ship was able to pass through without paying a fee to his agents.[6]

With the arrival of the clans of the Bani Ka'b in Falahiya, a township in Arabistan, the Musha'sha'aide dynasty began to decline after a rule that had endured for more than 500 years. Meanwhile the power of the Bani Ka'b dynasty[7] was growing and extending its sphere of influence to the north and east. The Bani Ka'b allegiance to the Ottomans and the Persians was dubious. Without actually submitting to either, the Ka'bides, in the midst of the conflict between the two parties, were able to prove themselves essential to the security and stability of the area; they were responsible for safeguarding navigation and trade in the Shatt al-Arab across the Arabian Gulf, since they used to guide the land caravans. This placed them in a position of strength between two rival empires which were competing for the friendship and allegiance of the Bani Ka'b.

Owing to the Bani Ka'b's geographical location on the Shatt al-Arab and the Gulf, their leaders earned their living (apart from their date-groves and other agricultural products) by building a large seagoing fleet which came to be considered one of the major fleets in the Arabian Gulf area during the eighteenth century. With this fleet they consolidated the independence of their young principality and dominated all the islands and shores of the Shatt al-Arab as far as the frontiers of Basra,[8] thus becoming a 'thorn in the side' of its Ottoman governors (Mutasallims) throughout the latter's rule.

The emergence of the Bani Ka'b fleet was, in fact, a momentous development. It was one of the major forces of the area, imposing its sovereignty over the northern part of the Gulf, while the al-Qawasim[9] dynasty were masters in the south. Thus the Arabian Gulf became a strictly Arab zone, free from any foreign influence.

Writers on the Bani Ka'b and the other tribes which dominated naval life in the Shatt al-Arab area and the Arabian Gulf, especially British historians, have described them as 'pirates' or 'brigands', a term that needs to be reconsidered.

The tide of tribes that flooded in from the Arabian peninsula forced other tribes to the shores of the Gulf, as the land could not feed them. One of those was the Bani Ka'b, which started to use small boats for fishing, pearl-fishing, and trading between the Arabian Gulf and Asia. They were situated in the middle of the eastern trade routes which run between the Indian Ocean and the

Mediterranean. Clearly, the area was too important to be left undisturbed.

Large European ships competed with the Bani Ka'b for the trade, their source of livelihood. Consequently, they were obliged to resort to the sea and to the same methods of conflict used among the land tribes. These conflicts became naval battles in which they successfully challenged the European ships. The same measures were employed by Portugal, Holland, France and England, and described by their initiators as naval engagements carried out on behalf of their countries.[10] Since, in that area, a tribe may be described as an official political entity, these naval encounters by the Arabs may also be described as attempts to prevent incursions by the Europeans into Arab territories.

These wars were not motivated by a desire to seize or annex foreign territory. They were launched in defence of the Arab character of the tribes' lands and their sovereignty over them. It was the legitimate right of the Bani Ka'b to resist foreign interference in these areas. Their wars, therefore, may rightly be considered as part of the historical Arab resistance movement in the Shatt al-Arab and the Arabian Gulf.[11]

There was remarkable activity by the Ka'bides in the Shatt al-Arab region during the reign of Shaikh Salman bin Sultan (1737–67), considered to be the greatest ruler in that area in the eighteenth century. He was depicted as a brave and intelligent man. During his reign, the Shatt al-Arab area flourished as never before. He encouraged agriculture and trade in all the regions under his rule;[12] he employed experts from Oman and reinforced the Ka'bide fleet, making it comparable in strength to the Ottoman fleet in Basra; he imposed taxes on all ships passing through the Shatt al-Arab and the northern part of the Gulf without exception; he defended the area by force, extending his authority over all the ports between Abadan island and the neighbourhood of Bushir; he crossed over to the right bank of the Shatt al-Arab, thus bringing it under his rule, and seized all ships in Basra and the islands near the mouth of the Shatt al-Arab.

The area under Shaikh Salman's authority also included Kerdalan, which is one of the dependencies of Basra. By occupying its port, his Emirate extended from Ahvaz to Bubyan island in the shape of a triangle of 100 miles on each side.[13] He attacked and harrassed foreign navigation in the Shatt al-Arab. His first threat was felt in 1747, when the East India Company's records reveal that Shaikh Salman attacked the ships coming into Basra, preventing foreign navigation in the Shatt al-Arab altogether.

Shaikh Salman was also a source of concern to the Ottoman authorities in Basra. The Mutasallim Ali Pasha felt obliged to maintain friendly relations with him, an attitude the East India Company also found prudent under the circumstances.[14]

Shaikh Salman himself was a man of great wisdom and a strong personality. During his reign, the Danish traveller Carsten Niebuhr visited Arabistan, and the book he wrote on his travels is now a valuable document. It describes Shaikh Salman's authority over the Shatt al-Arab area and his cleverness in dealing with the Persian Shah and the Ottoman Wali.[15] Niebuhr says that the Shaikh 'dominated all the islands and the mouths of the Shatt al-Arab which previously belonged to Basra'. He refused to pay taxes or tributes to the Persian Shah, Karim Khan, on the excuse that the Turks were extracting huge amounts from him, leaving him nothing with which to pay. When asked for money by the Turkish Pasha of Baghdad, he adopted the same tactic, but this time complained about the Persians. He knew how to attract the notables of Basra to his side, thereby annexing, one by one, the villages of the area to his domain. He levied considerable customs duties on the ships coming from Basra, and compelled them to buy his dates on their return voyages.[16]

Shaikh Salman's reign was marked by stability. He eliminated highwaymen and promoted security among the people throughout his reign, thereby enabling the economy, which depended on agriculture and trade, to flourish and prosper. One of his major contributions was the building of a dam to provide irrigation for the township of Sabila, on the Karun river, a great benefit to the people living on the surrounding lands.

As a result of this development and prosperity, and Shaikh Salman's complete domination over the area of the Shatt al-Arab, his young Arab Emirate attracted the envy and greed of neighbouring powers, eager for its riches.

The first outside attack on the Ka'bides came from Persia. Karim Khan the Zendi launched a ferocious attack on the Shatt al-Arab area in 1757, but it failed.[17] This failure by the Persians, however, did not deter the Ottomans from trying their hand. In an expedition prepared by the Mutasallim of Basra in 1761–2, in co-operation with the headquarters of the East India Company in Basra, a British ship (the *Swallow*) joined the Ottoman fleet in besieging the

Map 3.1: The Shatt al-Arab during the Ka'bide Period

Map 3.1

Note: Names of tribes are in italics.

Ka'bides' position on the Shatt al-Arab and the shores of the Arabian Gulf, especially in the Khor Musa area. Shaikh Salman retreated into his lands, leaving the attacking forces to face the empty shores and swamps, and the expedition was doomed.[18]

As a result of these defeats, the year 1765 witnessed an unusual alliance between the Persians and the Ottomans, aimed at destroying the Ka'bide Arab leader. They found the British ready allies. Each party had its own motives. The Persians, tempted by the economic and strategic importance of these Arab areas, hoped to annex them; the Ottomans wanted to extend their sovereignty over the Shatt al-Arab and levy duties on all ships passing through it. The British, having moved the headquarters of the East India Company from Bandar Abbas to Basra in 1763, needed to be on friendly terms with the Ottoman authorities. The Sultan had granted the Company a sort of diplomatic status, recognizing it as a political body and accepting its agent as British consul in Basra. It was advantageous to Britain, therefore, to maintain good relations with the Ottoman authorities in Basra, and when the Pasha of Baghdad requested British assistance in his war against the Bani Ka'b, Britain readily obliged. The Company's ships provided a guarantee of the presence of a British fleet in the Shatt al-Arab, and Ottoman reliance on the British naval force was an essential factor in the alliance.

However, Shaikh Salman, whose naval strength made him the undisputed master of the Shatt al-Arab, was prepared. His fleet consisted of some 100 ships of various sizes and types, and his forces were trained under his personal supervision. They were trained in such a way that they could fight on land, and could engage in battles in rivers and seas as well as in the swamps and marshes, and they were also skilled divers and snipers.[19]

In the spring of 1765 the alliance moved in different directions. The forces of Karim Khan besieged the Ka'bide Emirate from the north and the east, while the Ottoman forces were on the south and west. Lorimer relates that Shaikh Salman was a man of great military genius.[20] He broke the blockade with minimum losses and retreated from the forces marching against him across the Karun river. He customarily left towns empty of inhabitants and provisions, complicating the invaders' lives with starvation. The Persians sought help from the Ottomans as the situation deteriorated, but the Ottomans were themselves too weak to help. Each party accused the other of treachery. The British tried to help the Ottomans in their military preparations, but it seems their actions were without much consequence, especially as they came too late.[21]

Karim Khan considered the question of victory over Shaikh Salman and the occupation of his land to be a matter of Persian national honour, and later made special efforts to destroy the authority of the Shaikh over the Shatt al-Arab. He started by breaking down the Sabila dam, flooding the agricultural land on the left bank of the Shatt al-Arab and attacking the date-groves, thereby destroying the economic life of the Emirate. On the other hand, as Curzon relates, one of the tributaries of the Karun river turned into a dry valley as a result of this destruction.[22]

Shaikh Salman resisted, waiting for nature to take revenge for him on the Persian army. He went into hiding in the inland areas of Arabistan, and the Persians waited wearily. Meanwhile, the Ottomans repeated their attempts to attack the Shaikh's forts. A force of 5,000 strong marched towards Abadan, to where they transferred their headquarters in order to face the Ka'bides, but they were again too weak to achieve their aims.[23]

The Ka'bides faced these difficulties with patience and courage. The aggressor powers, tired of waiting, offered Shaikh Salman an armistice. Shaikh Salman consented, one reason being that his friend Mir Muhanna, Shaikh of Bandariq, urgently needed him to counter a British-Ottoman attack. Shaikh Salman considered it a duty of friendship to terminate his own dispute in order to fulfil his national duty towards a fellow Arab. Persian and Ottoman forces retreated without damaging Arab sovereignty over the Shatt al-Arab area.

The fate of the British followed that of their allies. The Ka'bides attacked the British ships, the *Sally*, the *Fort William* and others, blocked navigation in the Shatt al-Arab for them, and threatened British trade in the entire area. In spite of repeated attacks by the British navy, the Government of Bombay was not able to achieve a significant success. They then sent forces and ships to take part.[24] An expedition consisting of three large and three small ships, and a small garrison of infantry and artillery, arrived in the Shatt al-Arab in the spring of 1766. The Ka'bides attacked and seized the ships. The British Agent in Basra made several attempts to secure their return from Shaikh Salman by promises and the offer of various material rewards,[25] but the Arab Emir refused them all and ordered the ships to be burned.

The British then imposed a blockade over the waterway of the Ka'bides in the Shatt al-Arab. It lasted for two years, but the British eventually had to lift it because the blockading ships were rapidly deteriorating.[26]

The Bani Ka'b were thus independent and free from any foreign influence. For a long time, they were an annoyance to the Turks, the Persians and the British.[27] When the threats subsided, they started recovering their forts and reinforcing them on both banks of the Shatt al-Arab and launched repeated attacks on the Ottomans in Basra.

Their activities increased during the reign of Sulayman Agha, the Mutasallim of Basra, who was known as Sulayman the Great (1765–76). The Bani Ka'b threatened the security of Basra[28] and interrupted its trade, blocking navigation in the Shatt al-Arab by anchoring three ships across the river. In July 1773 their fleet attacked the house of the Kaputan Pasha, capturing some of the ships from his fleet. The Wali was obliged to purchase their friendship with money. In 1774, in the Shatt al-Arab, the Bani Ka'b captured the Ottoman ship *Faizi Islam* which belonged to the fleet of Basra, but it was rescued with the help of the British.[29]

The British, capitalizing on the Ottomans' situation in the Shatt al-Arab, threatened to withdraw unless granted additional concessions and compensation for their losses in the war with the Ka'bides. The Pasha of Baghdad agreed to bear all the expenses of the British fleet in the Shatt al-Arab in return for their protection of the Turkish fleet in Basra — this was at a time when the Pasha had scarcely any fleet to protect Basra and safeguard navigation in the Shatt al-Arab. The withdrawal of the East India Company's ships would have meant exposing Basra to the mercy of the Bani Ka'b. According to a letter written by the East India Company's Agent, 'The Pasha's influence and authority in Basra are only maintained thanks to the existence of British ships in the Shatt al-Arab.'[30]

Nevertheless, the Ottoman authorities in Basra were not completely safe from attack by the Bani Ka'b. After the death of Shaikh Salman, the Ka'bides allied themselves with Karim Khan and joined in a retaliatory attack on Basra led by Karim Khan's brother, Sadiq Khan, against the Ottomans and the British. Karim Khan was driven by his ambition to dominate Basra and later the Shatt al-Arab, which would have helped him dominate Oman also, the greatest part of whose trade was with Basra. Furthermore, it would have undermined the policy of the British Agent in Basra, which was to boycott the Persian ports, thus making Basra the principal centre for all trade in the region.[31]

Officials of the East India Company made every effort to prevent the Ka'bides' fleet from joining the Persians, but without success.[32] Lorimer remarked, 'Without the fleet of this tribe the Persian forces would not have been able to move.'[33]

It seems the Persians had actually recognized the strength of the Bani Ka'b (who were Arabs), and their sovereignty over the Shatt al-Arab. This was why, having failed to confront them unilaterally, they had asked them to join in attacking the Ottomans.

On 7 April 1775 the Ka'bides and the Persians were able to blockade Basra. A fleet of the Bombay navy was standing in the Shatt al-Arab. Wilson relates that the attitude of British merchants at the beginning was strictly neutral, but that the pressure of circumstances led them into the dispute. A fleet of 14 ships belonging to the Bani Ka'b made its way, secretly, to the north of the Shatt al-Arab.[34] In order to prevent their further advance, the British Agent, a Mr Moore, in co-operation with the Ottomans, built a barrier across the Shatt al-Arab to the north of the Ashar river consisting of large boats (used to transport passengers and cargo) tied together by chains and ropes. It was completed in two days (24 and 25 March) and was designed to prevent aid reaching the Persians and to block navigation in the Shatt al-Arab. This measure, however, did not deter the advance of the Persians and the Ka'bides, who broke through on 13 April 1775.

During the siege, help arrived from the Imam of Oman, Ahmad bin Said,[35] whose fleet took up position at the mouth of the Shatt al-Arab. The cruiser *Al-Rahmani* managed to break a chain placed by the Persians across the Shatt al-Arab. Thus once again the Ottomans were in control of the Shatt al-Arab and able to free it for navigation throughout the summer of 1775, thereby securing the arrival in Basra of all their needs. The Ottoman government awarded the Imam of Oman an annual subsidy[36] in appreciation of his gesture.

During the siege, the British had moved their Agency from Basra to Kuwait.[37] Their Agent in Basra, Mr Moore, had retreated from the battle to Bushir, taking with him the British ships and leaving the Company's headquarters and belongings unprotected. The siege continued for 14 months before the Ottoman forces in Basra surrendered.[38] This weakened further the Ottomans' presence in Iraq, which was already under the influence of the Mamelukes.[39]

Sadiq Khan then set out to build a strong fort on the left bank of the Shatt al-Arab opposite Ashar,[40] but when the news of his brother's death reached him he retreated from Basra. His place was taken by the Arab tribes of Muntafiq, who drove out the remaining Persians.[41]

The Ka'bides continued as an active power, posing a constant threat to other powers in the region. In 1782 they attacked areas belonging to Basra on the eastern banks of the Shatt al-Arab, and captured some important parts of it.[42] In 1783 the Bani Ka'b attacked the Omani fleet which carried the yearly supply of coffee to Basra, but the attack did not succeed and the Ka'bides suffered severe setbacks. Although they attempted to block the fleet's passage on the return voyage, no major confrontation took place. In retaliation for this defeat, the Bani Ka'b established several bases on both banks of the Shatt al-Arab.

From this time onwards, the Ottoman authorities regarded the Bani Ka'b with concern and dismay because they had dared to establish bases on Ottoman lands on the east bank of the Shatt al-Arab, and had demanded compensation for the losses suffered as a result of their attempted attacks on the Omani fleet. The matter, however, ended there.

In 1784 war broke out again between the Bani Ka'b and the Ottoman authorities in Basra. The Ka'bide leader, Ghadhban bin Muhammad (1782–92), succeeded in capturing all the lands on the east bank of the Shatt al-Arab as far as the village of Kerdalan. He even settled Ka'bide men on the western bank of the Shatt only ten miles away, to the south of Basra. He was in a position to capture Basra itself, but did not do so for fear of attacks on his estates.

The succession of victories raised the morale of the Bani Ka'b and extended their influence over the entire area of Arabistan. It seems that the Ka'bides were constantly in touch with the other Arab tribes in Qatar, Bahrain, Kuwait and Oman. There, is however, no evidence that there was ever a formal alliance among these tribes, and the subsequent disappearance of Arab sovereignty over the Arabian Gulf can be largely attributed to this fact.

A significant event in the political life of the Emirate then occurred: a sharp conflict arose in the ranks of the Emirs, leading to a serious schism. The Ka'bide leader had granted permission to Mardaw bin Ali bin Kasib, Shaikh of the Albu-Kasib tribe (one of the clans of the Bani Ka'b), to settle at the mouth of the Karun river, and one of their Emirs (Haj Yousuf) had laid the foundations of the city of Muhammarah in 1812. This marked the beginning of the division of the Bani Ka'b into two sections: one (the Albu-Nasir) remained in Falahiya,[43] while the other (the Albu-Kasib) moved to Muhammarah.[44] But Muhammarah became an enemy instead of a supporter of the Falahiya section of the Bani Ka'b.[45]

The section remaining in Falahiya was also divided, in 1849, over the question of the Emirateship. War erupted between the two factions, and the Persians seized the opportunity to attack.

However, they subsequently left Haj Jabir bin Mardaw, the leader of the Albu-Kasib at the time, to settle the dispute.

The most outstanding event involving the Persians after this concerned Ghaith bin Ghadhban (1812–29), one of the Shaikhs of the Bani Ka'b. Shaikh Ghaith came under strong Persian pressure, and asked the Sultan of Muscat and Oman, Said bin Sultan, to send land and naval forces to eliminate the Persian threat to his independence;[46] Persia abandoned its efforts. As to the authorities in Basra, they proved totally unable to confront the growing power of the Bani Ka'b. The Mutasallim of Basra, Aziz Agha, sought help from the Shaikh of Kuwait, Jabir al-Sabah, to halt their continuous attacks. Muhammarah and Abadan were attacked in 1827, and the Ottomans succeeded in capturing the village of al-Barim (Abadan) and confiscating all of its date crop. The war ended with negotiations between Shaikh Ghaith and the Wali, Daoud Pasha.[47] The Ottoman authorities in Basra were compelled to turn a blind eye to the situation as the price of their friendship.

The Shatt al-Arab had acquired even greater importance after the founding of the town of Muhammarah in 1812. It became a commercial port for the ships destined for Persia and Kuwait, and was able to compete with the only Iraqi port on the Shatt al-Arab, Basra.[48] The following were all factors in the Ottomans occupying Muhammarah: the competition between Muhammarah and Basra; the attempts to solve the dispute as to which side Muhammarah belonged and the enforcement of Ottoman sovereignty over it; the continual attacks on Basra by the Bani Ka'b[49] (the last attack taking place upon the dismissal of Daoud Pasha, the last Mameluke Wali in Iraq); and the Ottoman government's distrust of the Bani Ka'b. An additional inducement was that the Shah was busily engaged in the siege of the city of Harat in Persia.[50] The Laz Ali Ridha Pasha[51] heeded the advice of M. Fontanier, France's roving consul. Fontanier persuaded him to occupy Muhammarah, one of the centres of Anglo-French rivalry in the area, lest the British get there first.[52]

Fontanier became Ali Ridha's political and military adviser during the operations.[53] Ali Ridha led an expedition towards Basra in 1837 and was joined by some Arab tribes. In Basra he was joined by Shaikh Jabir al-Sabah of Kuwait and his forces, and together they attacked Muhammarah with land and river forces.[54] After a three-day battle, Ali Ridha Pasha captured the town, and the forces of Haj Jabir bin Mardaw (the Shaikh of Muhammarah) retreated.

Ali Ridha destroyed the town's forts and houses and killed many of its people. Falahiya, the capital of the Bani Ka'b, was not spared; its Shaikh, Thamir bin Ghadhban (1832–7), fled to Hindiya, leaving in his place Abdul-Ridha bin Barakat as the Emir of the Bani Ka'b.[55]

As to Muhammarah, Ali Ridha had left without appointing an Ottoman ruler, organizing its administration or attaching it to Basra. For that reason he was criticized and his campaign described as a raid to 'loot and run'.[56]

Ali Ridha returned to Kuwait accompanied by Shaikh Jabir al-Sabah, who had helped him consolidate his influence over the Shatt area and save Basra from the Bani Ka'b.[57] His success was short-lived, however. Haj Jabir bin Mardaw returned to Muhammarah, and once there, decided to meet Ali Ridha in Kuwait. The two men agreed that Haj Jabir should be in charge of Muhammarah without interference from the Ottoman government, which accepted the Haj's symbolic allegiance.

From the above, it is obvious that the leaders of the Bani Ka'b constantly refused to abandon their sovereignty in favour of Persia or the Ottoman Empire. It also appears that the region's links with Iraq, and especially with Basra, were stronger than those with Persia. Geographical, historical and demographic factors are powerful elements conducive to intermixing. The eastern parts of the Shatt al-Arab are open to Iraq, while Persia is cut off by high mountains which form a strong barrier that is difficult to cross.[58] As to tribal relations between the Bani Ka'b of Iraq and the Bani Ka'b of Arabistan, they can hardly be overlooked or over-estimated. They are relations of blood, race, affinity, language and destiny.[59] Therefore, it is not to be wondered at that a firm social and economic interchange exists between Basra and Arabistan. Intermarriage occurs between peoples of the two regions due to the strong ties. Thus it has become impossible to separate them. Furthermore, many people in Basra acquired large estates on the left bank of the Shatt al-Arab,[60] and they paid rates and dues on them to the Ottoman government. This is why the region of the east Shatt al-Arab was considered an integral part of Iraq,[61] and was included in the boundaries of the Wilayat of Basra.[62]

After the Ottoman occupation of the Bani Ka'b's Emirate, Persia, fearing an encirclement by Ottoman forces from the south and west, interfered in the matter and protested. They sent Menujehr Khan (Mu'tamad al-Dawla, the Governor of Fars) to the east bank of the Shatt al-Arab on various pretexts. These were: Shaikh Thamir bin Ghadhban's failure to send provisions for his army; and Shaikh Thamir's failure to hand over Muhammad Taqi Khan, the chief of the Bakhtiari tribes, who had taken refuge with him when he declared a mutiny against the Qajari state. Mu'tamad al-Dawla finally occupied Arabistan (1840–2) and Shaikh Thamir fled from Hindiya to Kuwait.

Menujehr Khan first installed Abdul-Ridha bin Barakat as Emir over the Ka'bides, but he later ordered that al-Mawla Faraja-lah al-Musha'sha'i be appointed governor of Falahiya.[63] When the Ottoman authorities refused to hand over Shaikh Thamir, he exerted great pressure on the Bani Lam. Shaikh Thamir was obliged to flee to Ottoman lands, and the Persian tribes of Failies descended from their mountains to attack the camps of Bani Lam.[64]

In addition, Persia demanded compensation for the losses inflicted by the Ottoman forces upon the Emirate, and the two nations, exhausted by prolonged wars, were forced to negotiate.[65] Furthermore, Britain, with an eye on Ottoman lands, and Russia, which sided with the Persians, interfered. These two powers pressed the conflicting nations to accept them as mediators in solving the dispute, which became dangerous in 1842 after the appointment of Najib Pasha (1842–7) as Wali of Baghdad. Najib Pasha was determined to impose Ottoman sovereignty over all the areas whose loyalty to the Sultan was in doubt. He threatened Persia with Shaikh Thamir, who was a refugee with the Ottomans. The Persian reaction was a new demand for the east bank of the Shatt al-Arab as far as Qurna[66] to be annexed to Persia. A battle almost erupted between the two parties, but Russia and Britain interfered, and a quadripartite committee was formed to reach a solution.[67]

Britain put forward proposals for the boundaries between the two states, but the Russians refused.[68] The British attitude was expressed in Lord Aberdeen's objection to the annexation of Arabistan to Persia, because Britain wanted the Karun area opened for its commercial and naval enterprises.[69] After prolonged meetings, lasting over a three-year period, the committee's work came to a halt owing to the attack by Najib Pasha's forces on Karbala in 1843. The Persians used this as a political negotiating card.[70] One of their demands was compensation for the losses and damages inflicted on Arabistan during Ali Ridha's occupation of

Muhammarah. The Sultan replied by requesting that they withdraw from Muhammarah. The crisis intensified, and the Ottoman government sent a battleship to the Karun river in 1846 to divert trade from Muhammarah to Basra, whose trade had all but vanished. The battleship forced all ships sailing towards Muhammarah to pass through Basra and pay a customs duty before being allowed to proceed. Persia objected and was supported by Britain.[71] The battleship had to be withdrawn.

When the parties in dispute found that the settlement of the boundary issue would require a long time, they preferred to conclude a treaty which solved some of the existing problems, leaving the remainder for further consideration at a later time. The outcome was the Second Treaty of Erzerum on 31 May 1847, concluded during the reign of the Ottoman Sultan Abdul-Majid and the Persian Shah Muhammad.

Notes

1. For detailed geographical and historical information on the Bani Ka'b see: W. F. A. Ainsworth, *Personal Narrative of the Euphrates Expedition* (Kegan, London, 1888), vol. 2; G. N. Curzon, *Persian and the Persian Questions* (Longman, London, 1892), vol. 2; C. Niebuhr, *Voyage en Arabie et en d'autre pays circonvoisins* (S. J. Baalde, Amsterdam, 1776–80), vol. 2; J. G. Lorimer, *Gazetteer of the Persian Gulf, Oman and Central Arabia* (7 vols., Superintendent of Government Printing, Calcutta, 1908–15), vol. 2.

2. Al-Qalqashandi, *Nihayat al-'Arab fi Ma'arifat Ansab al-'Arab* (The Golden Record in Arab Geneology) (Dar al-Bayan, Baghdad, 1958), p. 329. A secret British intellegence report states that the Bani Ka'b tribes are all of one origin, including the Ka'bides who are settled in Arabistan; while Abbas al-Azzawi suggests that there are still large groups of Ka'bides in Iraq. See his *Tarikh al-'Iraq bayna Ihtilalayn* (The History of Iraq between two Occupations) (Matbu'at al-Furat, Baghdad, 1935–56), vol. 7, p. 39.

3. S. H. Longrigg, *Four Centuries of Modern Iraq* (Clarendon Press, Oxford, 1925), p. 78.

4. Ibid., p. 41. He also mentions the Emir of Howaiza, saying that he is the representative of an old Arab line, probably connected with the Rabi'ah.

5. Abd al-Karim Gharaybah, *Muqaddima fi Tarikh al-'Arab al-Hadith* (1500–1918), vol. 1, p. 99.

6. The Ottomans, however, were not happy about this control, so they tried to annex the areas belonging to the Ka'bides after the battle in which the armies of Shah Abbas I were defeated near Baghdad in 1587. See Khuzistan in *The Encyclopaedia of Islam*, vol. 5, p. 38.

7. Ainsworth, *Euphrates Expedition*, vol. II, p. 208; A. T. Wilson, *The Persian Gulf* (Allen & Unwin, London, 1928), p. 187. The Ka'bides are said to be the descendants of the Bani 'Amir bin Sa'sa'a. They took as their capital the city of Qiyan in Arabistan which belonged to the Ottoman Empire and was occupied by Afrasiyab, the ruler of Basra since 1595. The first Emir of the principality was

Shaikh Ali bin Nasir al-Ka'bi, who became ruler in 1690. This year may be considered the start of the Arab principality. The move to Falahiya took place in 1747 under the leadership of Shaikh Salman bin Sultan.

8. Abd al-Amir M. Amin, *Al-Quwa al-Bahriyah fi al-Khalij al-'Arabi fil-Qarn al-Thamin Ashar* (Naval Powers in the Arab Gulf during the Eighteenth Century) (Matb'at As'ad, Baghdad, 1966), p. 41.

9. The al-Qawasim were famed for their prowess in naval warfare. They descended upon Oman in the second half of the seventeenth century and belong to an Arab tribe. Their origin goes back to Adnanides and they come from Samarra in Iraq. They settled in their new homeland and showed superior strength in the eighteenth century, taking Ras al-Khaima as their headquarters. Britain, France and Holland entered into an alliance against them, and Britain was able to dominate their region in 1819, forcing them to sign the treaty of 1820 which stipulated the forming of the seven Shaikhdoms of the 'Trucial Coast'. See a detailed report in Selection of the Records of Government of Bombay, no. 24 (Bombay, 1856), pp. 290–359. Also see S. B. Miles, *The Countries and the Tribes of the Persian Gulf* (2 vols., Harrison, London, 1919), vol. 2, p. 269.

10. Mustafa al-Najjar, *Al-Tarikh al-Siyasi li-Imarat 'Arabistan al-'Arabiyah* (A Political History of the Arab Principality of Arabistan) (Dar al-Ma'arif, Cairo, 1971), pp. 44–5.

11. Mustafa al-Najjar, *Al-Tarikh al-Siyasi Limushkilat al-Hudud al-Sharqiyah lil-Watan al-'Arabi fi Shatt al-Arab* (A Political History of the Problem of the Eastern Boundaries of the Arab Homeland in the Shatt al-Arab) (Jam'iyat al-Difa' 'an 'Urubat al-Khalij al-'Arabi, Basra, 1974), pp. 47–59.

12. '. . . he encouraged agriculture, repaired the dams and perfected the system of irrigation, protected caravan tracks . . .', Curzon, *Persia*, vol. 2, p. 323.

13. Salih Mohammad Al-'Abid, 'Imarat Ka'ab al-'Arabistaniyah' in *Al-Hudud al-Sharqiyah lil-Watan al-'Arabi* (The Eastern Boundaries of the Arab Homeland) (Baghdad, 1981), p. 231.

14. Rasul al-Kirkukli, *Dawhat al-Wuzara fi Tarikh Waqai' Baghdad* (History of Baghdad) (Dar al-Katib al-'Arabi, Beirut, 1963), *passim.*

15. Niebuhr, *Voyage en Arabie*. This author may be considered the best source on the Shatt al-Arab area and the Arabian Gulf in the eighteenth century. He lived in the area for the period 1764–5, leaving important and accurate historical and geographical information and maps. He stated that the area and its surroundings were Arab with no Persian influence.

16. *Mushahadat Nibur fi Rihlah min al-Basrah ila al-Hillah, 1765* (Niebuhr's Observations during his Journey from Basra to Hillah in 1965), translated from German into Arabic by Su'ad Hadi al-Umari (Dar Ma'rifah, Baghdad, 1955), pp. 35–6.

17. John Malcolm, *The History of Persia* (John Murray, London, 1815), vol. 2, p. 76.

18. John R. Perry, 'The Bani Ka'b: An Amphibious Brigand State in Khuzistan' in *Le Monde Iranien et l'Islam*, Tome I (Droz, Geneva—Paris, 1971), pp. 136–7.

19. Ibid., p. 137.

20. Lorimer, *Gazetteer*, vol. 1, pt. II, pp. 1628–9.

21. Perry in *Le Monde Iranien*, pp. 139–40.

22. Curzon, 'The Karun River and the South West Persia' in *Persia*, vol. 2, pp. 343–4.

23. Perry in *Le Monde Iranien*, p. 141.

24. For information about these battles see Lorimer, *Gazetteer*, p. 1639.

25. For details see Amin, *Al-Quwa al-Bahriyah fi al-Khalij*, pp. 46–7.

26. A. M. Abu-Hakimah, *Tarikh Sharqi al-Jazirah al-'Arabiyah: Nashaat wa Tatawwur al-Kuwait wal-Bahrain* (The History of the East Arabian Peninsula: the

Emergence and Development of Kuwait and Bahrain), translated from English into Arabic by Muhammad Amin Abd Allah (Dar Maktabat al-Hayah, Beirut, 1966). p. 113.

27. A. T. Wilson, *The Persian Gulf: An Historical Sketch from the Earliest Times to the Beginning of the Twentieth Century* (Allen & Unwin, London, 1928), *passim*.

28. With the exception of a short period of good relations between the Bani Ka'b and the Ottoman authorities in Basra. The Basra authorities aided the Ka'bides against the Muntafiq by lending them 14 ships in the autumn of 1769.

29. Gharaybah, *Muqaddima fi Tarikh al-'Arab*, p. 146.

30. For details of the campaigns against the Bani Ka'b, see the chapter on Arabistan in Lorimer, *Gazetteer*, pt. I.

31. Strangley enough, Abu-Hakimah in his thesis on the History of East Arabia refers to Muhammarah during and before this time (pp. 57, 118, 119 and 134) while Muhammarah did not exist and was only built in 1812. See al-Najjar, *Al-Tarikh al-Siyasi li-Imarat 'Arabistan al-'Arabiyah*, p. 90.

32. For an idea about the warships used by the Ka'bides, the Ottomans, the British and the Persians at that time see *Mashayikh Ka'b fi al-Qaban wal-Dawraq* (The Shaikhs of the Ka'b Tribe in the Qaban and the Dawraq Areas), Appendix II, p. 105.

33. Lorimer, *Gazetteer*, pt. I, p. 1850.

34. Wilson, *The Persian Gulf*, p. 45.

35. The reason for his taking part was that Karim Khan had asked the Turks for assistance during his war with the Imam, a request which they had turned down. Now the Imam wanted to express his gratitude to the Turks by rushing to their aid.

36. Salah al-Aqqad, *Al-Tayyarat al-Siyasiyah fi al-Khalij al-'Arabi* (Political Trends in the Arab Gulf) (Maktabat al-Anglo al-Misriyah, Cairo, 1965), *passim*.

37. Abu-Hakimah, *Tarikh Sharqi al-Jazirah*, p. 128.

38. Ali Zarif al-A'zami, *Mukhtasar Tarikh al-Basrah* (Brief History of Basra) (Matbu'at al-Furat, Baghdad, 1927), p. 143.

39. For additional information see Ja'far Khayyat, *Suwar min Tarikh al-'Iraq fi al-'Usur al-Muzlimah* (Sketches from the History of Iraq during the Dark Ages) (Beirut, 1971), vol. 1, pp. 187–96.

40. Ashar is the present village of Kerdalan. The word means 'the high land'. The Persians made it a military centre.

41. Abd al-Aziz Sulayman Nawwar, *Tarikh al-'Iraq al-Hadith min Nihayat Hukm Da'ud Pasha ila Nihayat Hukm Midhat Pasha* (The History of Modern Iraq from the end of the Reign of Daoud Pasha to the end of the Reign of Midhat Pasha) (Dar al-Katib al-'Arabi, Cairo, 1968), p. 23.

42. Lorimer, *Gazetteer*, vol. 1, pt. II, p. 1945.

43. See Appendix I in al-Najjar, *Al-Tarikh al-Siyasi li-Imaraat 'Arabistan al-'arabiyah*, for a list of the names of the Emirs of the Bani Ka'b (Falahiya section) until the downfall of their Emirate.

44. Abd al-Fattah Ibrahim, *'Ala Tariq al-Hind* (On the Road to India) (Baghdad, 1935), p. 14; Darwish Pasha, *Report on the Demarcation of the Iranian-Ottoman Boundaries*, p 4; Abd al-Qadir Bash-a'yan, *Tarikh al-Basrah (History of Basra). Shaikh Khaz'al was the last Amir Albu-Kasib in Muhammarah.*

45. Ahmad al-Sufi, *Al-Mamalik fi al-'Iraq* (The Mamelukes in Iraq) (no publisher, Mosul, 1952), *passim*.

46. Mahmoud Ali al-Da'ud, *Ahadith an al-Khalij al-'Arabi* (Notes about the Arab Gulf) (Baghdad, 1960), p. 17.

47. Husayn Khalaf Shaikh Khaz'al, *Tarikh al-Kuwayt al-Siyasi* (Political History of Kuwait) (Matba'at Dar al-Kutub, Beirut), vol.1, pp. 78–81.

48. Ahmad Kisrawi Tabrizi, *Tarikh band Sale Khuzistan*, p. 181.

49. Bash-a'yan, *Tarikh al-Basrah*, vol. 2, p. 348.

50. Kisrawi, *Tarikh band Sale Khuzistan*, p. 182.

51. Laz Ali Pasha of Trabzun, one of the Ottoman ministers, held various posts before rising to the rank of minister and Wali of Aleppo. Upon the overthrow of Daoud Pasha in Iraq, he became Wali of Baghdad (1813–41), then was transferred to Damascus where he died.

52. Fontanier was appointed French consul in Basra after the overthrow of Mamelukes in Iraq, and played an important role in keeping his government informed about the conditions and the general situation in Iraq and Arabistan and the extent of British influence there.

53. Fontanier, *Voyage dans l'Inde et le Golfe Persique par l'Egypte et la Mer Rouge* (Paulin, Paris, 1844–51), vol. 1, pp. 374–5.

54. Muhsin al-Amin, *A'yan al-Shi'a* (Notables of the Shi'a), vol. 15, pp. 193–5; Muhammad ibn Khalifah al-Nabhan, *Al-Tuhfah al-Nabhaniyah fi Imarat al-Jazirah al-'Arabiyah* (The Nabhani Treasures about the History of the Arabian Peninsula) (no publisher, Mecca, 1913), vol. 9, p. 314.

55. Al-Azzawi, *Tarikh al-'Iraq bayna Ihtilalyn*, vol. 7, p. 38.

56. Ibid., p. 40.

57. Jamal Zakariya Qasim, *Al-Khalij al-'Arabi* (The Arab Gulf) (Jami'at 'Ayn Shams, Cairo, 1966), p. 20.

58. M. Sykes, *History of Persia* (Macmillan, London, 1921), vol. 2, p. 366.

59. Abd al-Karim al-Nadwani, *Tarikh al-'Amara wa'Asha' iriha* (A History of Amara and its Tribes) (no publisher, Baghdad, 1961), p. 72.

60. The house of Kawawiza owned more land in Arabistan than any other family. See Bash-a'yan, *Tarikh al-Basrah*, vol. 11, p. 343.

61. Wilson, *The Persian Gulf*, p. 42.

62. Ibrahim Fasih al-Haydari, *Ahwal al-Basra* (The Condition of Basra) (Dar al-Basri, Baghdad, 1961), p. 27.

63. Ali Ni'mah al-Hilu, *Tarikh Imarat Ka'b al-'Arabiyah* (A History of the Emirate of Ka'b), pp. 92–6.

64. Nawwar, *Tarikh al-'Iraq*, p. 332.

65. The Persian and Ottoman governments concluded a series of treaties concerning the boundaries, the most important ones being:

(1) The treaty of Qasr Shirin during the reign of Sultan Murad IV in 1639 (whereby the Safavid state finally recognised Iraq as being a part of the Ottoman Empire).
(2) The treaty of Nadir Shah in 1727 (whereby Howaiza district entered into the sphere of the Ottoman Empire).
(3) The treaty of Nadir Shah in 1746 (which was a confirmation of the previous treaty of 1639).
(4) The First Erzerum Treaty of 1823. (At the time, this was considered one of the most important documents. However, it did not solve the dispute finally, as many points were left pending, especially the problem of Arabistan.) See the texts of the treaties in Shakir Sabir al-Dabit, *Al-'Alaqat al-Dawliyah wa Mu'ahadat al-Hudud bayna al-'Iraq wa Iran* (International Relations and Boundaries between Iraq and Iran) (Dar al-Basri, Baghdad, 1966), pp. 29–62.

66. Nawwar, *Tarikh al-'Iraq*, p. 333.

67. Mahmud al-Durrah, *Al-Qadiyah al-Kurdiyah* (The Kurdish Question) (Dar al-Tali'ah, Beirut, 1963), pp. 64–5.

68. Ibid., p. 65. Russia was trying to open the area of Karum and south-east Persia to its influence in order to reach the warm waters.

69. Lorimer, *Gazetteer*, vol. 1, pt. I, p. 1375. Owing to the importance of Arabistan for British commercial interests and for the lines of communication,

Taylor (the British consul in Baghdad) informed the British ambassador in Constantinople of the developments in the situation in Arabistan, although it was not easy to discover the truth about the situation.

70. It seems that the Persians exaggerated the crisis in Karbala and made several demands on the Ottoman Government. On these demands see Nawwar, *Tarikh al-'Iraq*, p. 337.

71. Lorimer, *Gazetteer*, pp. 1378–80.

4 OIL AND THE IRAN-IRAQ WAR

David E. Long

One of the scenarios most commonly heard over the last decade for the disruption of the entire oil market has been the prospect of a war between two or more Gulf oil producers. Because of their long history of mutual antagonism, Iran and Iraq were the most likely candidates: one is a radical, Arab, Sunni-dominated state, with a large Shi'a population; the other is conservative, Persian and the heartland of Shi'ism. Historically there has been little love lost between the two countries. Recent confrontations involving the demarcation of the Shatt al-Arab, and Kurdish irredentism on both sides of the border were the subject of a settlement in 1975, but underlying tensions remained just beneath the surface. The Iranian revolution saw Iranian-Iraqi relations plummet. Then, in September 1980, the doomsday scenario became nightmarish reality. Iraq attacked Iran.

The immediate impact of the war was to shut off virtually all oil production by both countries. Iraq quickly announced that it would refrain from attacking economic targets (in other words, oil), but Iran's response was to attack Iraqi installations. Iraq soon answered in kind. Thus, almost from the start, each side attempted to cut off the economic life-blood of the other. The Iraqis attacked Iran's refinery at Abadan and off-loading facilities at Khorramshahr, Bandar Mahshahr, Kharg island and Ras Behregan. Iran countered with attacks on the Iraqi refinery at Basra, off-loading facilities at Fao, Khor al-Amaya and Mina al-Bakr, and, in the north, on the key K-1 pumping station in the Kirkuk field.

Within a week of the outbreak of fighting, Iraq was forced to suspend virtually all exports, and Iran's were reduced to little more than a trickle through Lavan and Sirri island down the Gulf. Iraqi production for October 1980 was 500,000 b/d, down from an average of 3.4 million b/d, or 12.3 per cent of OPEC production for the first nine months of 1980. Iranian production dropped from an average of 1.8 million b/d, or 6.7 per cent of OPEC production for the same period to a mere 350,000 b/d. This represented a drop of roughly one sixth of total OPEC production.

Almost immediately after the war broke out, the spot market began to rise. Oil traders prepared for the worst. Yet the worst never happened. Almost three years have passed and, far from having an adverse effect on the oil market, the war has actually been seen by some as a godsend, easing what has become one of the greatest international oil gluts in recent years. In fact, a speedy end to the war — admittedly still an unlikely prospect — could have a more profound effect on the market by increasing the current glut, than the outbreak of the war did in creating a shortage.

In order to examine this ironic set of circumstances, it is necessary to go back to the years preceding the Iran-Iraq war. Although few realized it at the time, the world oil markets (the terms of whose trade had been turned upside down by the Arab oil embargo and the energy crisis of the early 1970s) were seeking a new equilibrium. It was not an equilibrium, however, destined to give comfort to either buyers or sellers. In short, the oil market had entered a period of sharply accelerating and decelerating cycles.

Of course, the oil market had always been affected by normal business cycles in the world economy, but prior to the energy crisis of the early 1970s, oil producers were able to maintain market equilibrium. This was accomplished in great measure by the major oil companies, which since the 1920s had co-operated in balancing oil supply and demand internationally, and also by the Texas Railroad Commission which performed roughly the same function domestically in the United States.

Since the 1970s, however, oil markets have not only become more responsive to international business cycles, they are a major contributing factor towards them. In oversimplified terms, OPEC solidarity enhanced the upward climb in oil prices during tight market periods beyond the point which the world economy would normally have supported. At the point at which the world economy could no longer support such prices, demand would soften and an oil glut would ensue. As the world economy recovered, oil demand would pick up and the process would start all over again.

Higher energy prices since 1973–4 have set in train several developments which have further disrupted oil market stability. One has been the more efficient use of oil, which has softened over-all demand quite apart from recurring economic cycles. Even if the real price of oil decreases substantially in future years, there is no reason to believe that energy-saving technology will be abandoned.

A second factor is the shift to alternative sources of energy such as coal for electricity-generating plants. Unlike the days when the Texas Railroad Commission regulated domestic US oil prices, OPEC did not monitor prices to discourage a shift away from oil. On the contrary, many oil-producing countries were convinced that the shift was a good thing, since oil was a wasted asset; with high world inflation, 'oil was worth more in the ground'.

The shift to alternative sources would probably have been greater had not the capital costs involved been so high. Due to the extremely low production costs for Middle East oil (roughly $1 per barrel), alternative sources would always be under the threat of being undercut in a price war with oil. The threat is even greater when one considers that, with approximately five years' lead, Saudi Arabia could probably increase productive capacity from between 10 and 11 million b/d to 18 million b/d, leaving the alternative suppliers with white elephants. Even coal production, which is relatively cheap in the United States, has incurred huge environmental protection costs in recent years; in Europe, extraction costs are much higher to begin with.

An additional result of higher oil prices has been the expansion of non-OPEC production. Not only has oil that was previously too expensive to recover become commercially exploitable, but the rapid price rises of the 1970s also set off a worldwide search for new sources: North Sea and Mexican oil are two prime examples. Non-OPEC producers, while benefiting from OPEC price rises, have not been subject to OPEC self-discipline in setting price and production rates, adding a further element of market instability, particularly in periods of glut.

Another factor brought on by higher oil prices has been the propensity of most oil-producing countries to expand government expenditures faster than rising revenues, particularly in the late 1970s and early 1980s. In 1974 the producers had foreign exchange holdings large enough to make threats of production cuts credible. Since then, virtually every producer except Saudi Arabia, and perhaps one or two other Gulf states, has run up huge deficits with lavish spending programmes. This situation has not only made the OPEC price hawks more anxious to increase prices in tight market conditions but has also made the financially over-extended producers desperate to maintain revenue levels. The current glut has thus further undermined efforts to stabilize prices and market shares.

The demand side of the severe market fluctuations of the late 1970s and early 1980s, however, appears to have been less affected by economic factors than by psychological factors. As demand rapidly outstripped supply, due to major oil disruptions, or exceptionally tight market conditions, or both, panic buying became an almost irresistible temptation. Because most crude oil transactions are on long-term contracts which are relatively insulated from panic buying, upward pressure on prices was felt initially on small, short-term or 'spot' transactions of a single oil-tanker load or less. However, long-term contractors also had an adverse effect on the spot market. Concern among companies buying Iranian crude began to rise during the oil workers' strikes in October 1978, and even though production was soon restored (albeit at a somewhat lower level), British Petroleum and Shell began to cut back on third-party sales (crude sales to other oil companies) to preserve supplies. As a result, the other companies were forced onto the spot market, causing it to rise even higher. The panic psychology was also manifested in government-to-government and government-to-company sales and barter arrangements, which tended to by-pass the spot market but nevertheless placed additional upward pressure on prices.

The rising spot market, however, rather than acting as a brake on demand, actually fuelled further panic buying. This not only resulted in even higher spot prices, but was ultimately exploited by OPEC to establish higher posted prices for all transactions. Thus, each successive perceived shortage tended to result in a higher price level than could be supported on strictly economic grounds, setting the stage for a subsequent market crash and oil glut.

Another psychological factor that has had a profound effect on the oil market involves stockpiling. The oil industry has stockpiled crude and product inventories for years, in order to meet seasonal fluctuations in demand. Following the Arab oil embargo of 1973–4, however, a concerted effort was made in the major consuming countries to build up stocks of strategic reserves as insurance against another major oil disruption. The logic of building strategic reserve stockpiles was that, immediately following a disruption, a timely draw-down of stockpiles could dampen the effect of the sudden shortage, both in terms of providing interim supplies and in psychological terms of simply knowing it was there. It was also seen as a possible deterrent to politically induced disruptions, the so-called oil weapon.

This type of insurance has not been without its price, however: it has intensified the volatility of the cyclical behaviour of the international oil market. As inventories were drawn down below normal seasonally adjusted levels, there would be an increasing pressure to restock. This has usually happened on an upward price cycle, and the added demand for restocking has helped to push prices even higher. Inevitably, overpriced crude has contributed to a weakening of the world economy even more than might have been the case, thus creating a recession, the severity of which has tended to push demand even lower than it otherwise would have been. Conversely, in periods of declining demand, holders of large inventories tended to draw down. First of all, there was less fear of being denied assured market access to crude in a declining market than in a rising market. Secondly, stockpiling is expensive. In recent years particularly, high interest rates have added an extra burden to the costs of maintaining large inventories. And finally, it was expected that cheaper replacement stocks could be purchased as the glut bottomed out.

In a falling market, it might appear good business to sell expensive stocks, lower storage costs, and then restock when the market bottoms out. Compelling as this logic is, however, it has resulted in companies and countries building up inventories in a rising market and drawing down inventories in a declining market. The result has been to sharpen the peaks and valleys of the market cycles, an economically destabilizing practice, despite any possible short-term commercial gains.

The most visible factor playing a major role in the post energy-crisis oil market has been the recurrence of major production disruptions. It has been these disruptions which, more than any other influence, have given rise to panic buying and strategic stockpiling. The first disruption was the Arab oil embargo of 1973–4, the second was the Iranian revolution of 1978–9, and then in 1980 there was the Iran-Iraq war itself. In all three cases, the market reacted to what was perceived to be a sudden shortage by resorting to a net draw-down of stocks at the outset, followed by the building of inventories.

Table 4.1 shows the relationship between inventories and price run-ups for these three crises. As the table indicates, there was a net destocking in the first quarter of the Arab oil embargo, accompanied by a net restocking in early 1974 as prices rose from $5.18 to $11.34 per barrel. As a result of the Iranian revolution, net

Table 4.1: Impact of Major Supply Disruptions of Oil Stocks and Oil Prices

	Primary oil stocks Rate of change (mb/d)			Oil prices[a] ($ per barrel)
	Actual	Normal	Net	
Arab oil embargo				
1973 4th quarter	− 1.5	− 1.0	− 0.5	$ 5.18
1974 1st quarter	− 0.9	− 1.5	+ 0.6	11.36
2nd quarter	+ 4.5	+ 2.0	+ 2.5	11.34
Iranian revolution				
1978 4th quarter[b]	+ 0.1	− 0.3	+ 0.4	$12.91
1979 1st quarter	− 4.4	− 3.1	− 1.3	13.79
2nd quarter	+ 2.6	+ 2.2	+ 0.5	17.08
3rd quarter	+ 4.3	+ 3.4	+ 1.1	20.14
4th quarter	+ 0.9	− 0.6	+ 1.3	23.55
Iran-Iraq war				
1980 3rd quarter	+ 2.5	+ 2.6	− 0.1	$31.74
4th quarter	− 2.2	−0.9	− 1.3	32.61
1981 1st quarter	− 1.8	− 3.6	+ 1.8	34.84
2nd quarter	+ 1.8	+ 2.0	− 0.2	34.65

Notes: a. OPEC: average crude oil official sales price.
b. Government-owned stocks increased by 600,000 b/d.
Source: US Central Intelligence Agency.

destocking in the first quarter of 1979 was followed by net restocking in the succeeding quarters. Prices nearly doubled, rising from $12.91 to $23.55 per barrel.

The Iran-Iraq war appeared at first to follow the same pattern, but by the second quarter of 1981, it was obvious that there would be no price run-up and that the glut was likely to extend well into the 1980s. The difference was based on a number of factors.

First, unlike the previous two disruptions, the Iran-Iraq war occurred on the down side of a market cycle. Indeed, the Iranian revolution was in great measure responsible for this. By January 1979, the eve of the advent of the Iranian Islamic Republic, Iranian production had dropped to just 445,000 b/d from 2.3 million b/d in December and 6 million b/d in September 1978. The Iranian revolution created panic buying, which resulted in the doubling of oil prices in 1979. By the outbreak of the Iran-Iraq war in September 1980, they had reached an average of $31.74.

By January 1980, however, world demand had already peaked,

and right up to the outbreak of the Iran-Iraq war was gradually declining. In the first nine months of 1980, OPEC production declined from 29.9 million b/d to 25.4 million b/d, a net drop of 4.5 million b/d. World production during the same period dropped from 64.9 million b/d to 61.3 million b/d, a net drop of only 3.6 million b/d. The difference was made up by non-OPEC sources, an added depressant to the market. Table 4.2 compares Iranian, Iraqi, OPEC and world production for the years 1978–82, showing market fluctuations for this period.

With demand softening, there was plenty of excess production capacity within OPEC to compensate for the disruption of Iranian and Iraqi production. Moreover, to nearly everyone's surprise, Saudi Arabia announced in October 1980 that it would increase production from 9.5 million b/d to 10.4 million b/d to ease the crisis.

Finally, with Saudi Arabia producing well over its own previously stated 'ceiling' of 8.5 million b/d, world stocks had built up to record levels. It was estimated that, at the time the war broke out, non-communist world stocks had reached between 4 and 5 billion barrels. Only about 1.1 billion barrels could actually be considered for emergency draw-down, the rest being minimum operating stocks, pipeline fill, and so on. Nevertheless, this was a huge amount.

As a result of this combination of factors, the perceived 'loss' of about 4 million b/d from Iranian and Iraqi production caused the average price of OPEC crude to rise from $31.74 to $34.64 per barrel by 1981. In retrospect, the main impact of the outbreak of the Iran-Iraq war on world prices was simply to delay for about a year the full effect of the glut.

The Impact of the War on the Soviet Union and other Communist States

The war has not affected communist oil and gas supply arrangements as greatly as if the Soviet Union had been a net oil importer. The prospect of the Soviet Union becoming a net importer is still in the future and the date of its occurrence is still debated by those who follow Soviet oil developments. It is interesting to speculate on what might have happened had the Iran-Iraq war seriously disrupted both communist and non-communist markets.

Table 4.2: Iran, Iraq, OPEC and World Oil Production, July 1978–December 1982 (thousand barrels per day)

Year and month		Iran	Iraq	OPEC	World
1978	Jul	5,848	2,400	29,401	63,301
	Aug	5.847	2,650	29,945	63,131
	Sep	6,093	2,900	32,048	65,266
	Oct	5,540	3,000	31,960	65,275
	Nov	3,493	3,100	31,775	65,722
	Dec	2,371	3,097	30,536	64,580
1979	Jan	445	3,097	28,461	62,004
	Feb	700	3,304	28,987	62,930
	Mar	2,350	3,300	30,388	63,961
	Apr	3,600	3,300	30,649	64,636
	May	4,097	3,300	30,992	64,679
	Jun	3,900	3,517	31,058	65,044
	Jul	3,806	3,500	31,870	65,713
	Aug	3,500	3,500	31,213	65,452
	Sep	4,000	3,500	31,535	65,767
	Oct	3,790	3,500	31,179	65,581
	Nov	3,250	3,667	31,099	65,937
	Dec	3,097	3,700	30,830	65,942
1980	Jan	2,700	3,500	29,902	64,919
	Feb	2,700	3,500	29,945	64,807
	Mar	2,500	3,500	29,161	64,516
	Apr	1,800	3,500	27,830	63,000
	May	1,400	3,597	27,390	62,742
	Jun	1,500	3,500	27,306	62,667
	Jul	1,500	3,400	27,084	62,419
	Aug	1,300	3,400	26,851	62,323
	Sep	1,100	2,900	25,457	61,300
	Oct	350	500	23,577	59,032
	Nov	500	500	23,918	59,467
	Dec	1,194	650	25,030	60,806
1981	Jan	1,194	650	25,060	60,774
	Feb	1,400	750	24,916	60,607
	Mar	1,750	950	25,243	61,161
	Apr	1,600	800	24,136	60,067
	May	1,500	900	23,288	59,194
	Jun	1,400	750	22,874	59,033
	Jul	1,400	900	21,765	57,097
	Aug	1,100	800	21,030	56,290
	Sep	1,000	1,000	20,762	56,467
	Oct	1,000	1,000	21,291	57,226
	Nov	1,000	1,100	20,828	56,700
	Dec	1,200	1,200	21,557	57,226
1982	Jan	1,100	1,300	20,916	56,903
	Feb	1,000	1,400	19,854	56,357
	Mar	1,100	1,200	17,877	53,710

Table 4.2: — *continued*

Year and month		Iran	Iraq	OPEC	World
1982	Apr	1,800	900	16,900	53,133
	May	2,500	700	16,900	53,355
	Jun	2,200	850	18,646	55,367
	Jul	2,400	900	18,580	55,194
	Aug	2,000	850	17,611	54,290
	Sep	2,300	800	18,133	54,500
	Oct	2,500	800	19,222	56,065
	Nov	2,600	800	19,315	n.a.
	Dec	2,750	800	18,624	n.a.

Source: Extracted from figures cited in the *Petroleum Economist* (1978–83).

Many observers have assumed that the Soviets anticipate a shift to becoming net importers at some point, and that as this happens, East-West competition for Gulf supplies will intensify. Such a situation could increase the probability of another major structural rise in the cost of energy, and with it, the chance for Soviet-inspired political subversion and political and economic blackmail. In such an environment, the likelihood of East-West conflict over a major oil disruption would be high. On the other hand, the prospects for East-West co-operation in restoring the flow might be enhanced simply because of perceived mutual interest. The prospects of the US and the Soviets co-operating in assuring the flow of oil is generally not as comforting to the Gulf states as one might suppose, since it could greatly reduce their power for independent manoeuvre.

In the case of the Iran-Iraq war, the Soviets had to look elsewhere to replace the oil they had been purchasing from Iraq and reselling in the Indian Ocean to meet commitments there. Iranian gas supplies to the Soviet Union were also cut off, but since the USSR is also a net exporter of gas, the problems associated with this were minimal, confined mainly to distribution. In sum, dislocations from the Iran-Iraq war did not seriously disrupt communist supply arrangements.

The Impact of the War on the Iranian and Iraqi Domestic Oil Sectors

The physical damage to both sides has been extensive. Nevertheless, it is now apparent that initial estimates of damage to oil installations were somewhat exaggerated. Even the damage to the oil-wells at the off-shore Nowruz field in early 1983, creating a monumental oil spill, is more disastrous environmentally than technically. The magnitude of the spill and the cost of a clean-up could add substantially to the financial burden of both countries. The most vulnerable installations in the fields themselves, gas-oil separating plants (GOSPs), escaped with minor damage. Moreover, air attacks by both sides have proved relatively ineffective. The most devastating damage has been sustained either in conjunction with the fighting around Abadan, or as a result of Iranian commando raids on the Iraqi off-shore terminals at Mina al-Bakr and Khor al-Amaya and on the pipeline which extends from Iraq through Turkey. The real damage caused by war to Iranian and Iraqi oil sectors, therefore, has been less in physical damage than in lost revenues. These losses are particularly acute, in view of the rapidly escalating costs of sustaining the war effort on both sides. It is impossible to estimate the ultimate total loss in revenues, but it could well run into hundreds of billions of dollars.

The over-all effect of the war on Iran's oil sector has been much less devastating than on that of Iraq. Nevertheless, the destruction of the Abadan refinery was a serious blow. In fact, damage to refineries has turned both countries into net importers of refined products. Although the loss of the Abadan refinery caused refined product exports to cease, it did not affect Iranian crude exports. The primary off-loading facilities at Kharg island have been damaged far less than was originally supposed. Not only have air raids been relatively ineffective — Kharg is sufficiently distant from Iraq to limit the effectiveness of air attacks — but redundancies are so extensive that the Iranians have generally been able to bypass whatever damage has been sustained. (Kharg has a capacity of 6 million b/d.) Thus, after an initial period in which production was almost halted, Iranian production climbed back up almost to immediate pre-war levels of around 1.5 million b/d. It then fell somewhat in late 1981 and early 1982 as the market softened and Iran began to encounter difficulties in marketing its crude (for example, it lost its Japanese market).

Iraqi production also recovered, but at a much slower rate. By September 1981 it had reached 1 million b/d and gradually edged upwards to 1.2 million b/d by March 1982. Iraq's production was constrained by the loss of its two major off-loading terminals in the

Gulf. Khor al-Amaya with a pre-war capacity of 1.8 million b/d, and Mina al-Bakr, with a capacity of 2.5 million b/d, were both destroyed by seaborne commando attacks early in the war. The pipelines supplying the terminals were not destroyed and could soon be hooked to floating loading buoys which are now sitting in Bahrain. But so long as the war continues, the Iraqis cannot begin work on replacing these facilities.

Quite apart from physical damage to Gulf terminals, it was initially feared that the threat of damage would frighten tankers away from the northern Gulf. The Iranian seizure of a Danish ship in the summer of 1981 and the more recent Iraqi raid on Kharg island have exacerbated those fears. In fact, both sides have 'guaranteed' free passage in the Gulf. This has helped Iran more than Iraq, since only Iran at present has off-loading capacity in the Gulf. Were Iraq to repair its facilities, the problem of the danger to ships using Iraqi terminals might, of course, arise again.

The closure of its Gulf terminals forced Iraq to rely exclusively on its pipelines to the Mediterranean. The pipeline through Turkey, with a capacity of 700,000 b/d, has subsequently been repaired. The other pipeline, through Syria (the old Iraq Petroleum Company pipeline), has a capacity of 1.4 million b/d. The Syrian pipeline had long been unreliable, however. Its Tripoli (Lebanon) terminal had been closed due to the 1975/6 Lebanese civil war, leaving only the terminal at Banyas in Syria. Moreover, due to bad relations between Iraq and Syria, the Syrian pipeline had been closed intermittently over the past several years, and there had been virtually no maintenance performed on it. Despite all these problems, Iraqi production continued to rise, reaching 1.4 million b/d by February 1982.

At this time, however, politics dealt Iraq another blow. Syrian-Iraqi relations, traditionally bad as each Baathist regime challenged the orthodoxy of the other, took a turn for the worse. Syrian President Hafez al-Assad took the unprecedented step of breaking Arab ranks by openly siding with Iran in the Iran-Iraq war. His decision may have been influenced in part by confessionalism. The largely Sunni town of Hama had recently risen up against the Alawite regime in Damascus and been put down only with brutal fighting. Assad seems to have been convinced that Iraq was some-how involved in the uprising. In any event, Syrian Foreign Minister Abd al-Halim Khaddam visted Tehran from 13 to 17 March 1982, during which time he signed a ten-year trade agreement. A month later, Syria closed its borders with Iraq and also closed the pipeline. That left Iraq with only the pipeline to Dortyol, Turkey.

It is interesting to note that as Iraqi production dropped off sharply in April and May 1982, Iranian production increased. This underscores the purely economic aspects of Iranian and Iraqi oil production as they are affected by the war. Iran, while it has been able to maintain production at pre-war levels, has a far greater need of oil earnings to maintain its economy and the war effort. Without the extensive foreign aid that Iraq is receiving, oil revenues are Iran's principal source of foreign exchange.

Short of cash, the Iranians have been trying to market their crude in any way possible. Their strategy has worked to some degree, as witnessed by the regaining of Japanese contracts for some 180,000 b/d in mid-1982. The Iranians have also been trying to take over Iraq's customers, particularly since the cut-off of Iraqi crude through Syria. As a result, Iraq has been attempting to buy Saudi crude for resale to its customers: while Iraq would make no profit, at least it would not lose its customers entirely.

Iraq has been able to avoid economic disaster and still finance its war effort mainly through generous subsidies from the Arab Gulf states, the total of which is estimated to be in excess of $25 billion. The Arab Gulf states' aid to Iraq has won them the ire of Iran and led to the continuing possibility of an Iranian attack on Gulf oil installations. Although Iran has denied it, it attacked some non-oil facilities in Kuwait in October 1981. Thus, Iran's relations with its Gulf neighbours both politically and through OPEC, are likely to remain bad so long as the war drags on.

A Balance Sheet

The overall damage done to the economies of the two antagonists as a result of the war has been astronomical, with the combination of lost revenues, damage to oil and other installations, and the tremendous financial burden of the war effort already reaching into the tens of billions of dollars.

Neither the Iran-Iraq war nor the oil glut had ended by the spring of 1983, and neither showed signs of doing so immediately. To the degree that Iranian and Iraqi oil has remained off the market during the period of glut, the war has actually injected an element of stability into the world oil market. If the war outlasts the glut, however, this situation could be reversed. A period of world economic recovery and rising demand for oil, and the denial of Iranian and Iraqi crude to world markets, could contribute to yet another disruptive oil shortage, with an accompanying round of price hikes beyond what normal market conditions would support, and the whole shortage-glut cycle could begin again.

The continuation of the war has also had a highly destabilizing effect on relations within OPEC. In its efforts to raise revenues, Iran has openly disregarded OPEC price arrangements, seeking to increase its market share by undercutting its OPEC partners. This has caused a downward pressure on prices which was only offset by Saudi Arabia's policy of dropping production from a high of 10.5 million b/d in 1981 to less than 4 million b/d in early 1983. When the Saudis indicated that they would no longer reduce production, and called on OPEC to lower prices, Iranian intransigence in demanding a higher market share was a leading impediment to OPEC's reaching a new agreement. An agreement to reduce prices by $5 per barrel was reached in March 1983, but it could still be undermined by several factors. The possibility that Iran will not restrict production in line with the agreement remains a major one.

The Arab Gulf producers' subsidies to Iraq are also a potential destabilizing factor for the international oil market. As oil revenues decline, the subsidies to Iraq will be increasingly more difficult to sustain, but will continue to be politically and strategically imperative from the Arab point of view. The Gulf producers are in the soundest financial position of virtually all the OPEC producers, but if the decline in revenues resulting from the oil glut continues, the financial burden of the subsidies to Iraq could become an important factor in the Gulf states' oil policies.

There can be no question that the ending of the war would be a great economic boon to both Iran and Iraq and to the region generally. The April 1983 negotiations, aimed at securing the co-operation of all the Gulf states in halting the oil spill, could be used as an avenue toward such an end. Despite indications that Iraq would be amenable to this idea, Iran has insisted that it has no intention of linking the oil spill to an overall ceasefire. Rarely in history have short-term political goals been driven by economic interests. Unfortunately, the Iran-Iraq war appears to be no exception.

5 ECONOMIC AND POLITICAL IMPLICATIONS OF THE WAR: THE ECONOMIC CONSEQUENCES FOR THE PARTICIPANTS

John Townsend

Harsh necessity, and the newness of my kingdom, force me to do such things.

(Aeneid i, 563)

Just as war can be regarded either as an extension or as a failure of a nation's foreign policy, so can the economic consequences of a war be either apocalyptic or cathartic for a nation and its people. The longer-term economic consequences are incalculable at the moment when a nation's political leaders make the calculation, or the miscalculation, which takes foreign policy into war. Few German policy-makers in the late nineteenth or early twentieth century could have even dimly envisaged the decades of catastrophe which they were conjuring, decades which ultimately created, however, the environment and the motivation for an 'economic miracle'. The cost of this 'miracle' in terms of human suffering was enormous, almost unparalleled in the history of mankind.

The over-used expression 'economic miracle' was employed to describe France after the defeat of 1870–1. The spur of heavy reparation payments and the bitterness of defeat caused a proud people to exert themselves and rebuild their national economy over two decades, stronger eventually than it was on the eve of political miscalculation which led to war. Yet few who surveyed the ruins of the national economy in the dark days of the commune in Paris in the spring of 1871 could have envisaged the rapid economic renaissance of the nation.

Thus the task of describing, forecasting and analysing the economic consequences for the participants in the current round of the Shatt al-Arab dispute is particularly daunting. There is an added difficulty in the case of Iran, of course, in that this country's economy had already been severly disrupted by the revolution which overthrew the Shah. Apart from specific war damage, it is virtually impossible to say that this economic effect was caused by

51

the war whereas that economic effect followed a revolutionary cause. Even the fearful toll of battle casualties is more or less matched, according to some estimates at least, by the flow of blood from executions and terror as the revolution first destroyed its enemies and then devoured its children.

A further difficulty is caused by the absence of reliable data. Even at the best of times, the governments of both Iraq and Iran had not earned international reputations for the quality and availability of their national accounting statistics. An understandable concern to keep vital data from one's enemy, coupled with an inevitable degree of bureaucratic disruption from the war, means that a serious student of the economic environment today in both Iraq and Iran has to work very hard indeed for the scraps of information that come his way and be especially careful in appraising them.

This article looks briefly at each country's major economic activity, its oil industry, which leads to foreign exchange earnings and the ability both to sustain economic development and to import the goods and services required or expected by the individual nation and its people. As others in this book will be looking at each country's oil industry, this article will mention only oil production totals and annual export earnings. The article goes into more detail on foreign trade and economic development programmes. It will consider briefly the manpower situation and the effects of the war so far on domestic markets and prices and will try to look ahead at some of the possible consequences of the war which may emerge in the years ahead. Inevitably, at this time and in these circumstances, such an article can aim only to focus on probable trends and possible consequences; definite conclusions are not possible.

Table 5.1 summarizes Iranian and Iraqi oil production over the five-year period 1978–82 inclusive, a period which, of course, embraces both the Iranian revolution and the beginning of the war between Iran and Iraq.

Table 5.1: Iran and Iraq, Oil Production, 1978–82 (million barrels per day)

	1978	1979	1980	1981	1982
Iran	5.2	3.2	1.5	1.3	2.0
Iraq	2.6	3.5	2.6	0.9	1.0

Source: *Petroleum Economist*, vol. L, no. 3 (March 1983).

Political agitation before the fall of the Shah had already contributed to a reduction in Iranian oil production. In *The House of Saud*, Richard Johns writes that, 'Iranian exports had slumped from an average of over 5 million barrels a day during September 1978 to about 1.5 million in December. Then the flow stopped completely.'[1] The war has not touched significantly Iran's capacity to produce oil at the pre-war (though not necessarily at the pre-revolutionary) level. At the July 1982 OPEC meeting in Vienna, the Iranian Oil Minister was quoted as saying that his country was going to try to increase exports to over 3 million b/d as soon as possible. Oil industry sources put Iranian exports at that time at marginally more than 2 million b/d. Whatever war damage has been caused to Iran's oil export terminals, this damage is clearly not great enough to impede exports seriously. Whether the terminals could handle the 5.7 million b/d being exported before the revolution is a somewhat academic point, given the damage to production facilities caused by the revolution and also given the weakened state of the international oil market.

The consequences for Iraqi oil production, and especially oil exports, are immediately much more serious. Production facilities appear to be relatively undamaged, but the export terminals at Fao, Khor al-Amaya and Mina al-Bakr are apparently seriously damaged. Even if they were unscathed, the possibility of exporting oil from the mouth of the Shatt al-Arab for as long as the war continues, or until such time as the dispute is settled, cannot be considered a strong option. For as long as the Syrian frontier is closed, Iraq can only export oil through Turkey, and at a rate of about 700,000 b/d.

Thus a very obvious economic consequence of the war for Iraq has been to emphasize the country's vulnerability to the closing of its vital export links. This vulnerability has been translated into projects for building a pipeline across Saudi Arabia to a Red Sea terminal north of Yanbu and to increasing the capacity of the pipeline through Turkey.

Of even more vital importance than a capacity to export oil, although obviously linked to this capacity, is the ability to generate foreign exchange. Table 5.2 totals Iranian and Iraqi export earnings for the five-year period 1977–81 inclusive.

As far as Iran is concerned, the revolution, for practical purposes, wiped out the country's foreign exchange reserves, so that the need to export to earn foreign exchange became paramount.

Table 5.2: Iran and Iraq, Exports, 1977–81 ($ million)

	1977	1978	1979	1980	1981
Iran	21,858	22,450	19,290	14,394	10,169
Iraq	10,377	11,932	20,310	28,608	9,372

Source: *IMF Directory of Trade Yearbook* (1982).

The effect of the war has been, of course, to increase the demand for foreign exchange but also to give great incentive to import substitution industries, especially for small arms and ammunition manufacture, tank and truck repairs and a whole range of small industries feeding and supplying the army. An additional incentive and stimulus to the domestic economy has come from the very strong xenophobia in Iran, and the determination to throw off any dependence on foreign technicians for key industries such as oil production and export, and the metal-working industries which support the army. Historically Iran has had a crafts and artisan tradition, and the strong entrepreneurial spirit of the people has thus led to the growth of a number of small workshops meeting the demands of the army and the marginally wider domestic market.

The same spirit has not served to revive the large-scale heavy industries, especially steel and petrochemicals. These relics of the grandiose dreams of Muhammed Reza Pahlevi were casualties of the revolution, not of the war. Even if there had been no war, these industries would not have been reborn. Given the depressed state of the steel and petrochemical industries worldwide, there must be a large question mark over the Iranian wish to pick up these relics of headlong economic growth masquerading as development.

Notable among the projects to which the war gave an added incentive is the Esfahan refinery. The destruction of the Abadan refinery, an old and increasingly inefficient establishment, has in some ways been a blessing.

When the war with Iran started in September 1980, President Saddam Hussein was widely quoted as having said that Iraq faced the war with two years' supplies of all key commodities. It seems that this was an accurate statement of the position, certainly as far as foreign exchange was concerned. Iraq started the war with substantial foreign exchange reserves. A consensus among interested foreign bankers at the time was that the country's foreign exchange reserves, including gold, totalled just under $30 billion when the war started. The government of Iraq maintains the greatest secrecy about its exact reserve level, a secrecy understandable in wartime, given the critical importance of the information. The conservative Arab oil producers of the Gulf region — Saudi Arabia, Kuwait, Qatar and the United Arab Emirates — provided, at least up to mid-1982, substantial financial support for Iraq. The result was that there was no serious shortage of foreign exchange until October 1982, and all foreign contractors and suppliers either working in or doing business with Iraq were being paid regularly and promptly up to that date. As long as the Arab brothers kept paying, Iraq was able to maintain healthy foreign exchange reserves, but as these support payments dwindled and appeared to stop in the summer of 1982, so Iraq's foreign assets began to slide dramatically.

The Bank for International Settlements suggested in its 1982 report that Iraq's foreign exchange holdings at the end of 1981 were $15.9 billion. The best estimates among foreign bankers put the total of aid received from the Arab brothers by mid-1982 at between $22 and $25 billion; the precise figures were naturally never disclosed.

Beginning in October 1982, foreign contractors and suppliers began to experience severe delays in payment. Prior to that date, Iraqi officials had begun to try to maximise the local currency element in all foreign contracts. In October, the Iraqi dinar was devalued by a government decision which received very little publicity. At the same time, the government approached a number of foreign banks seeking a major loan. Eventually a consortium of ten banks — two American, one French and seven Arab — were able to put together a $500 million syndicated package which was not signed until the second quarter of 1983. Most of the banks involved agreed privately that they had misgivings about the loan and that the syndication had necessitated a well-above-average effort on their part.

Hence a major economic consequence of the war has been the almost complete erosion of Iraq's foreign exchange reserves, reserves which were extremely healthy, covering perhaps two years' imports at normal rates, on the eve of the war. Given the major uncertainties in the international oil market in the 1980s, and hence major uncertainties in Iraq's ability to generate substantial foreign exchange surpluses again from oil exports for the next few years, it becomes apparent that this element in the cost of the war is likely to be very high, a cost whose economic impact may well continue to be felt for a number of years.

Turning to the import side of the foreign exchange equation, Table 5.3 sets out totals of Iran's and Iraq's imports over the five-year period 1977–81 inclusive. (The figures for 1981 are for the first six months only.)

Table 5.3: Iran and Iraq, Imports, 1977–81 ($ million)

	1977	1978	1979	1980	1981
Iran	14,642	19,489	8,435	12,592	12,634
Iraq	4,481	4,212	9,990	13,920	18,907

Source: *IMF Directory of Trade Yearbook* (1982)

It is apparent that, in broad terms at least, the war has had a negligible effect on the imports of both countries and that the Iranian revolution caused a fall of over 50 per cent in the country's imports. The import figures do not, by and large, include arms and weapons. Both countries are heavily dependent on food imports, Iran's bill for food imports being in excess of $3 billion annually and that of Iraq in excess of $1 billion. Given the difference in population between the two countries, it is apparent that, in very broad terms, *per capita* food imports are about the same in each country.

It seems likely that the war would have increased the demand for imported food in each country, if for no other reason than that erstwhile agricultural labourers tend to form a large part of the armies of both nations; hence there has almost certainly been a grave shortage of manpower at critical periods in the agricultural calendar covering planting and harvesting of key crops.

Iraq's foreign exchange cushion has meant that the nation has not had the same incentive as Iran to develop import substitution industries to save foreign exchange for the war effort. Nor has there been any dramatic nation-wide increase in industrial productivity because of the war, though it is possible that the Iranian invasion of Iraqi territory might supply an incentive for such an upsurge. On the other hand, some Iraqi engineers wrought small miracles of innovation, especially in the early days of the war, to repair war damage to key installations, especially power generating facilities.

Iraq's relatively favourable foreign exchange position has meant, too, that the government could afford to encourage large numbers of foreign workers to come into the country to maintain the pace of economic development and to take the place of Iraqis fighting in the army. These foreign workers have been employed mostly in the construction and the services sectors, and less in agriculture. Irrespective of where they have been employed, they all remit money home in one way or another, with a consequent drain on foreign currency reserves. Thus one somewhat anomalous effect of the war on the Iraqi economy has been a sharp increase in the numbers of foreign workers in the country and a consequent additional burden on the country's foreign exchange reserves. Iraqi officials told the writer in Iraq in April 1982 that there were about 1,500,000 foreign workers in the country and that about half this number were from Arab countries.

The Iranian manpower situation is very different. With a population about three times that of Iraq, and a manpower pool approaching nine million people, Iran is rich in sons, so rich that the lives of young men can be poured out in costly infantry attacks on prepared Iraqi positions. Iranian political opponents of the government often exaggerate the unemployment position. For example, Mehrdad Khonsari, writing in the *International Herald Tribune* on 14 July 1982, said that 'the once prosperous economy now has five million unemployed'. This is just not so. First, the army and the Revolutionary Guards have a very great demand for manpower to replace battle casualties. Second, every mullah in every mosque has his 'establishment' of followers who are paid quite well for doing nothing very much. Third, the small workshops and artisan industries backing the war effort employ significant numbers of people, and fourth, the urban drift of recent years has proved to be a reversible phenomenon. Most Iranians have strong family connections in the country and can always go back to their villages and find some economic activity. Underemployment in rural areas has always been a problem and remains so, but the war has not caused it. Nor does the war explain why many Iranians with good, often Western, technological qualifications have to accept the most menial of manual labour simply because they are politically 'unacceptable'.

It would be extraordinary if the war had not had some effect on markets, on distribution and on prices in both countries. Empirical visual evidence in both countries suggests that this is so and that some commodities, for example, motor fuel and cooking gas, have increased substantially in price in both countries, although Iraq would seem to be far less affected than Iran. Foreign embassies in both countries talk knowingly about rates of inflation of x% but almost all this sort of comment appears, on close analysis, to be little more than low-grade embassy dinner party circuit gossip. (In parentheses, it can be noted that one effect of the war in both countries has been to make foreign embassies even more isolated than they were in the pre-war days.)

The Iranian revolution put a stop to the country's development programme and the war, therefore, has had no effect on economic development for the simple reason that no economic development was taking place. It might be argued that, but for the war, the government in Tehran would have been able to start up a formal programme of development and revive some of the projects put into cold storage by the revolution. Although certainly not impossible, such conjecture seems improbable.

On the other hand, the government of Iraq made it clear right from the start of the war that the war was not going to impede the nation's development. Indeed, the government deliberately set out to accelerate the pace of economic development and went to considerable lengths in the first year of the war to ensure that the average Iraqi citizen would not suffer economically because of the war. Certainly up to the end of 1981 and probably up to the eve of the Iranian offensives of late March 1982, the Iraqi government was remarkably successful in attaining this objective. Indeed, history may judge that the policy was all too successful and may even have proved to be counter-productive in that a large number of Iraqis, probably the great majority, could not take the war seriously. Official Iraqi propaganda also removed any sense of national urgency by building up an image of Iraqi invincibility. Only those families who had lost sons, or whose sons had come home blind or maimed, knew anything of the reality of war. For the rest, there were no shortages that hurt, no pressure on prices, and after the first few weeks of the war, no air raids or threats of air raids. True, some commodities cost more, but not to the extent of causing hardship.

This policy, described as one of 'guns and butter' by one of the writer's colleagues, may have been the right option had there been a rapid and decisive Iraqi military victory in the first weeks of the war. But as the war dragged on, and as the numbers of new projects swelled in parallel (many of them obviously geared to the Non-Aligned Conference originally scheduled to be held in Baghdad in

September 1982), many critics of the policies of the Iraqi government began to argue that, had the resources being diverted to apparently prestige projects been concentrated instead on furthering the war effort, the Iraqi defeats of the spring and early summer of 1982 might have been averted.

This argument is the key to any serious discussion of the economic consequences of the war for Iraq. In broad terms, the total of contracts signed and announced by the government of Iraq (many contracts were kept secret) for projects, for the supply of capital equipment, food and some consumer durables such as private cars, and for some defence equipment, totalled $6,327.2 million in 1979, $14,821.8 million in 1980 and no less than $24,287.3 million in 1981. Another economic consequence of the war becomes apparent when one looks at the 1982 figures. A direct comparison is misleading, because the 1982 figures do not include contracts announced but with no value stated. Even if these contracts should add 20 per cent to the total (and empirical evidence suggests that this would be a high percentage), the total value of contracts signed by the government in 1982 would be considerably less than half the total signed in 1981. This would suggest that by the early part of 1982, at the latest, the government recognized that its earlier assumptions about the length of the war were wrong and that it would almost certainly have problems meeting its commitments. Again it should be mentioned that a great deal of the government's expenditures (but by no means all) was apparently geared to preparing the country in general, and the city of Baghdad especially, for the Non-Aligned Conference scheduled for September 1982. In the event, this conference was held in New Delhi in March 1983, but there is some hope that the 1986 conference will be held in Baghdad.

Table 5.4 sets out details of this public sector contractual spending over the three years 1980, 1981 and 1982, analysed by sector. This table has been derived from a research project carried out by Business International.

The important fact to be borne in mind is that all of the projects covered by the contracts summarized in Table 5.4 are proceeding. In all cases where the foreign contracting partner has to build or install equipment or physical infrastructure such as roads, railway or airport runways and public buildings in Iraq, the work in the country is continuing. All foreign contractors are being paid.

In other words, the Iraqi government's claim that, at least up to

Table 5.4: Iraqi Public Sector Contractual Spending, 1980, 1981 and 1982

Sector	Value of contracts reported ($ million)		
	1980	1981	1982
Agriculture and food: construction of farms, grain silos, fisheries and supplies of frozen and canned food.	539.8	510.2	177.3 (3 nvs)
Building materials: supply of building materials and construction of factories to manufacture and process these.	349	1,527	119.5 (4 nvs)
Civil aviation: construction, transport and equipment for civil airports, including aircraft and spares.	598.5	61.5	47.4 (4 nvs)
Civil engineering and roads: construction, preparation of ground, equipment for roads, bridges, expressways and related consultancy.	1,600.2	2,969.1	549.8
Construction/housing: all housing, whether civilian housing developments or military living quarters and officers' villas, public buildings, industrial zone building, and design and consultancy for all these.	1,579	2,695	239.6 (4 nvs)
Defence: armament supplies, including military vehicles and support services and military fabric such as aircraft aprons and runways, army colleges and training centres and facilities. DOES NOT INCLUDE WEAPONS.	300	3,873.6	3,160.0 (4 nvs)
Education: all educational buildings (except military), training schemes, training centres.	446.2	173.5	0.2 (2 nvs)
Health and social services: construction of all hospitals for civilian and military complexes, waste disposal contracts, cleaning services.	567.7	834.6	125.8
Hydrocarbons: all reported contracts for oil and petrochemical projects.	840.7	138.1	125.9 (2 nvs)
Irrigation/dams: contracts specifically defined as iriigation schemes or dam building.	595.4	2,188.6	596.9

Table 5.4: Iraqi Public Sector Contractual Spending, 1980, 1981 and 1982 — *continued*

Sector	Value of contracts reported ($ million)		
	1980	1981	1982
Port/river development: includes dredging and land reclamation specifically for ports, provision of ro-ro vessels, provision of all services for ports, construction of these, and management services.	428.1	545.1	27.9
Power: construction, installation, supply of all buildings, generators, switchgear and sub-stations for electrification schemes, any nuclear and solar energy schemes.	798.6	2,677.4	463.1 (6 nvs)
Public health engineering, water supply, sewage: all contracts for water supply schemes, including study projects and design, construction and provision of pipes, pumps and plant.	2,527	1,723.9	74.5 (2 nvs)
Railroads: construction and supply of rails, railway cars, engines and support services.	477.1	732.7	1,115.4 (2 nvs)
Telecommunications: all telephone and telex projects, TV circuits, national link system materials, tel-communication systems, Arabsat contracts.	1,518.8	953.8	60.3 (1 nvs)
Tourism, public amenities: sports complexes and other facilities, recreation areas, hotels, stadia and landscaping.	287.1	—	7.6 (3 nvs)
Transport: contracts not covered by military and civilian transport elsewhere — trucks and spares, bulk carriers, container vessels, shipping contracts, vehicle workshops.	554.7	1,033	363.6 (1 nvs)

Table 5.4: Iraqi Public Sector Contractual Spending, 1980, 1981 and 1982 — *continued*

Sector	Value of contracts reported ($ million)		
	1980	1981	1982
Other industry: construction of heavy industrial plant and equipment and factories not covered elsewhere, urban development schemes, basic industrial training, supply of manufactured goods and industrial equipment.	813.9	1,609	136.6 (3 nvs)
Total	14,821.8	24,287.3ª	7,391.4

Note: a. 1981 total includes $41.2 million of unclassified contracts.
Source: Business International Research.

the spring of 1982, the war had not slowed down the pace of economic development is reasonable. Furthermore, an analysis of these projects shows that by far the greater part are genuine economic development projects, adding to the nation's economic capital and contributing to the generation of future income.

In answering part of the question relating to the effects of the war on economic development in Iraq, one is, of course, as has already been suggested, posing a far more intriguing question. That is, what effect has the determination not only not to slow down, but on the contrary to accelerate sharply, the pace of economic development in Iraq contributed to the Iraqi army's inability to win a decisive victory in the war? There is no point in a country's political leadership taking it into a war unless a decisive victory is seen as possible. Decisive victories rarely come unless maximum strength is exerted. It can be argued, of course, that the Iraqi political leadership was not looking for a decisive military victory in September 1980, but rather for a political collapse in Iran — just as the British and the French hoped that an invasion of Egypt with limited military objectives in October 1956 would cause Nasser to fall from power. Intriguing as these thoughts are, they lead away from the main thrust of this article.

Historical analysis of nations at war throughout the centuries suggests that the true economic consequences of a war appear only after the last shot is fired and the earth thrown over the broken body of the last dead soldier. If the war were to end tomorrow, irrespective of victor and vanquished, each country would start the post-war period impoverished. The awful military jargon of 'body counts' suggests that over 60,000 young Iraqis have been killed or wounded, and probably over 100,000 young Iranians. Both sides hold prisoners of war. There are said to be over one million refugees from the province of Khuzistan in Iran, a province which has suffered considerable damage. The city of Khorramshahr is destroyed, the old oil refinery in Abadan will not produce again. (As mentioned earlier, this loss could be a blessing in disguise.) Again, history suggests that military victors often do not win great economic advantages for themselves, nor are the vanquished destroyed economically, in spite of grievous war damage. Britain emerged on the winning side in both World Wars, but with a seriously damaged economy, strained by the exertions of war. Germany and Japan, both completely defeated with their economies in ruins in 1945, were, a generation later, counted among the world's strongest economies.

If the present war could be brought to an end without apocalyptic consequences for either nation, then it is possible to hazard some guesses as to the possible longer-term consequences for each. This assumes, of course, that a degree of political stability is retained, that there is no occupation of large areas of territory by either side, that there is no civil war in either country, that there is no uncontrollable wave of social unrest and no general collapse. Perhaps this proviso is excessively optimistic. The longer the war drags on, the greater the risk of major disaster for either or both combatants.

But if this disaster can be avoided, what is the outlook for the economies of Iran and Iraq in the eventual post-war world? First, if there is any consensus at all among energy consultants as to future market trends in the international oil market, both countries will have considerable difficulty in maximizing oil production, or even in optimizing the use of existing production capacity. Again, that elusive consensus among energy economists suggests that the real price of oil, in 1981 dollars, will be marginally under $30 a barrel. A broad guess is that Iran would be able to export between 2.5 and 3 million b/d at this price up to 1985 and Iraq about 2 million b/d. Ir must be stressed that this is no more than a guess; every reader of this book could make his or her own guess and come up with figures which are not going to change the basic argument, which is that the days of cheap and abundant capital in both countries for investment in economic development projects are almost certainly gone for at least a decade. Both countries recognize this. This recognition lies behind the extravagant Iranian claim for reparations; it possibly lies behind the Iraqi government's determination to push ahead with development projects in spite of the war.

Both countries will face the post-war era with foodstuffs and agricultural and pastoral inputs (such as fertilizers and animal foodstuffs) having a very high priority in the use of foreign exchange. Both countries have a significant agricultural potential, but it is almost certain that agriculture will prove to be the sector most damaged by the war. This damage can be put right fairly easily, given the availability of manpower, the necessary inputs of capital, seeds, livestock and fertilizers. The greatest incentive to the reconstruction of the agricultural sector is likely to come from market forces, and the best thing that the governments of both countries could do to ensure this renaissance of their country's agricultural sectors would be to let market forces operate with minimum interference.

If the rightist trend in Iran's politics continues, then this free market economy concept could permit rapid recovery in the post-war era. The situation for Iraq is much more interesting. The rapid economic growth of the last decade in Iraq has taken place under an economic regime of a strong centralized public-sector *dirigisme*, with state control of markets and prices and a tightly controlled and restricted private sector. Some critics of Iraq's economy would say that the progress over the last ten years has been made in spite of the Iraqi bureaucracy. This article is not the place for a debate on the merits (or demerits) of the Iraqi bureaucracy. But it can be pointed out that there were signs immediately before the war of what was being described in government circles as 'an opening to the private sector'. President Saddam Hussein himself had said in various speeches that the government was withdrawing from direct involvement in the agricultural sector, the implied reason being that bureaucrats are not good farmers.

Thus it is possible to predict a very significant opening to the private sector in Iraq as part of a post-war reconstruction drive. The government would use the argument that the imperatives of reconstruction demand the complete mobilization of the nation as a matter of urgency, and that harsh necessity and the newness of the post-war society force it to move away from its socialist planning principles.

Note

1. David Holden and Richard Johns, *The House of Saud* (Sidgwick & Jackson, London, 1981), p. 507.

6 DEVELOPMENT STRATEGY IN IRAQ AND THE WAR EFFORT: THE DYNAMICS OF CHALLENGE

Basil al-Bustany

Introduction

In an independent economy, economic power generates military power and political leverage. Such economic power is governed by two sets of conditions. The first set relates to the degree of resource availability, human, material and financial. This constitutes its necessary condition. The sufficient condition is indicated by the second set, which involves the question of economic policy performance, in other words, the degree of success or failure in the allocation and use of these resources.

The economy of Iraq is endowed with an extremely balanced combination of resources. Its population exerts no real pressure on the land, where its agricultural potential far exceeds the country's population, supported by reasonably adequate water resources. Its fairly large mineral bases offer an excellent opportunity to build and sustain a broader industrial sector, both directly through the industrial potential of these minerals, and indirectly as a source of substantial development finance.

Consequently, Iraq possesses a reasonably adequate base of resources which would define it as a relative economic power. The necessary condition for such power is thus firmly established.

On the other hand, the securing of a more efficient utilization of resources for sustaining the development effort is in itself an obvious challenge which developing countries, including Iraq, continually confront. The task is made even more complex under the rising demands of the war effort. This has been the case in Iraq since the outbreak of hostilities with Iran in September 1980, when the interaction between the pressure of war and the response of economic policy was well exemplified, a question which this article attempts to examine.

The Background

Resources

Iraq has a fairly large, young and fast-growing population. With a total population of 13.1 million (1980), growing at an annual rate of 3.3 per cent, it constitutes 8.1 per cent of the total Arab population (estimated at 162.1 million in 1980), but exceeds that of all the Arab Gulf countries combined. Besides its fairly large population, it also possesses a well-educated and skilled labour force.

The potential of the agricultural sector is substantial, both in terms of abundant agricultural land as well as ample water resources. The magnitude of potentially cultivable land is estimated at over 12 million hectares, strongly supported by the petroleum industry which provides cheap fertilizers to increase fertility and thus production. And yet, at present, only 25 per cent of this potential in agricultural land is put to use, employing mostly sub-marginal methods of production.[1]

Before the start of the war, Iraq produced 3.7 million b/d of crude oil, second only to Saudi Arabia among Arab oil exporters, but now drastically reduced because of the war. In sulphur production, it ranks first in the Middle East region. The Mishraq field (the country's largest) produced 750,000 tons in 1979, but declined to 450,000 tons in 1980. The planned 1981—5 annual production was placed at 900,000 tons. Iraq also possesses large reserves of phosphate, where it was expected to emerge in 1982 as one of the five major producers in the Middle East. Total reserves were estimated at 1,760 million tons when the Akashat mine (the main reserves site) was inaugurated in April 1981, and annual production is 3.4 million tons.[2]

The Process of Structural Transformation

Obviously, the process of development, by its very nature, generates far-reaching socio-economic changes whose interaction characterizes the pattern of development itself. This is an established historical phenomenon which is experienced by all countries, industrial as well as developing, including the Arab countries.[3]

This process of structural transformation expresses itself in three major indicators, namely: the changing sectoral composition of the GDP; the changing labour force allocation among sectors; and the tendency towards urbanization. In Iraq, all these indicators were evident during the period 1960–80.

Changing GDP Sectoral Shares

Table 6.1: Structure of Iraqi GDP, 1960–80 (per cent)

Agriculture		Industry		Manufacturing		Services	
1960	1980	1960	1980	1960	1980	1960	1980
17	7	52	73	10	6	31	20

Source: World Bank, *World Development Report 1982* (Washington, D.C., 1982), p. 115.

From Table 6.1 we may note that:

(1) The relative share of the agricultural sector in the GDP lost substantial ground, as it declined from 17 to 7 per cent during 1960–80.
(2) The relative share of the services sector also declined noticeably, from 31 to 20 per cent.
(3) The decline in the relative shares of both the agricultural and services sectors was absorbed by the industrial (mainly extractive) sector, whose relative share increased from 52 to 73 per cent.

Sectoral Distribution of Labour Force. The change in the allocation of the labour force among sectors reveals some distinctive tendencies which differ markedly from those reflected in sectoral GDP shares. These include the following (Table 6.2):

Table 6.2: Iraqi Labour Force Sectoral Distribution, 1960–80 (per cent)

Agriculture		Industry		Services	
1960	1980	1960	1980	1960	1980
53	42	18	26	29	32

Source: World Bank, *World Development Report 1982*, p. 147.

Table 6.2 shows that:

(1) The increase in the industrial labour force was not completely effective in absorbing the relative decline in the agricultural sector, hence the rising relative share of the services sector.

(2) The slower rate of decline in the agricultural labour force, compared to the fall in its GDP sectoral share, no doubt implies rising underemployment in agriculture.

(3) The industrial sector was unable to absorb more labour, despite its dominance. The GDP demonstrates the pattern of factor-proportions prevailing in the sector: it is heavily capital-intensive, particularly in the extractive industries.

(4) The increase in the share of the services sector in the labour force reflects both the increased role of the public sector as well as rising underemployment.

Urbanization. During 1960–80, the percentage of the total population living in urban centres increased from 43 to 72 per cent. It is worth noting in this respect that, within a historical context, the tendency towards urbanization in the industrial countries differs markedly from the experience of today's developing countries. Whereas in the former, urban concentration came either in association — or mostly after — the process of industrialization had been firmly entrenched, in the latter, urbanization is taking place before establishing an industrial base. Consequently, the developing countries have succeeded in sharing the industrial countries' problems of modernization without reaping its fruits!

The External Sector

Judging by the level of this sector, Iraq's economy is heavily export-oriented. In 1980 the ratio of exports to GDP reached 74 per cent, that of imports 29 per cent, and the relative share of the sector (i.e. average exports and imports) amounted to 52 per cent.[4]

The balance of trade was strong during the 1970s, thanks to oil exports and revenues. Furthermore, this was augmented by positive terms of trade for most of the period. At the same time, however, elements of deterioration in the trade position have emerged, particularly in recent years. For example, while the average annual rate of exports during 1960–70 was 5.7 per cent compared with 1.4 per cent for imports, the situation was drastically reversed during 1970–80, when the rate of imports reached 20.5 per cent compared with only 2.2 per cent for exports (in real terms).[5] Further, while in

1979 the average annual percentage change in the value of exports reached 94.3 per cent compared to 66.2 per cent for imports, in 1980 the figures were 23.0 per cent and 86.2 per cent respectively. This switched the export-import ratio from 3.1 to 2.0 times between 1979 and 1980.[6]

Concerning the composition of foreign trade, exports are dominated by oil exports, making 99 per cent of the total. Machinery and transportation equipment comprise over 50 per cent of total imports, reflecting the intensity of the development programme.

Finally, the distribution of exports shows a substantial shift away from the industrial towards the developing countries. Thus, between 1960 and 1980, the relative share of the former declined from 85 to 61 per cent, while that of the latter increased from 14 to 39 per cent.[7]

Development Planning

Plan Objectives and Strategies

Successive development plans have generally advocated a number of common objectives, including the reduction of dependence on the foreign sector, and achieving self-sufficiency in food production. The achievement of these goals was to come through expanding the productive capability of both agriculture and industry, as well as building a more extensive base for the infrastructure, particularly in construction, transportation, electricity and services.

At the same time, however, more recent plans have distinctly emphasized two further objectives. First, paying particular attention to the development of human capital (in other words, education, health and social welfare), as well as attempting to mitigate the unfavourable impact of the development process on income distribution. And second, expanding and consolidating the role of the public socialist sector in directing economic activity. Thus by 1980 the government's share in sectoral distribution of GDP was 79 per cent for commodity, 48 per cent for distribution, and 78 per cent for services sectors. The corresponding sectoral fixed capital formation shares were 87 per cent, 86 per cent and 68 per cent respectively. Finally, the public sector share in foreign trade reached 91 per cent by 1980.

Development Expenditure Allocations

Investment allocations in the successive development plans are indicated in Table 6.3. The data reveal that: (1) a larger share of development expenditure is allocated to the industrial than to the agricultural sector; (2) in general, the relative shares of both these sectors have been declining in favour of other sectors, particularly construction and transportation.

Table 6.3: Iraqi Development Planning Expenditures, 1965–81

	I.D. million	Industry %	Agriculture %	Others %
Plan 1965–9	632	28	23	49
Plan 1970–74	1,932	20	19	61
Annual 1975ᵃ	1,076	42	19	39
Investment Prog. 1976	1,494	47	18	35
,, ,, 1977	2,377	41	16	43
Annual Plan 1978	2,800	29	18	53
,, ,, 1979	3,283	26	15	61
,, ,, 1980	5,240	22	10	68
,, ,, 1981	6,743	18	10	72

Note: a. Last eight months of 1975.
Source: Based on Ministry of Planning, *Annual Statistics, 1981* (Baghdad, 1982).

Development Performance

The GDP annual average growth rate (in real terms) during 1970–80) was very impressive: 12.1 per cent compared to 6.1 per cent for 1960–70. The GNP *per capita* increased by an annual average rate of 5.3 per cent (in real terms) during the 1960–80 period.[8]

On the other hand, GDP sectoral shares, show clearly the dominance of the commodity sector, whose relative share averaged over 77 per cent for 1973–80, followed by about 15 per cent for services and about 12 per cent for distribution, respectively. (Table 6.4).

One substantial increase in GDP growth rate, however, was not extended to the agricultural sector, which generally suffered from noticeable decline, both in relative and absolute terms. For besides its relative decline in GDP, its annual average growth rate of 1.7 per cent (as officially computed) was frequently subjected to

Table 6.4: Iraqi GDP by Sectors (factor cost; market price), 1973–81

	GDP[a] I.D. million	ISC I.D. million	Commodity I.D. million	%	Distribution I.D. million	%	Services I.D. million	%
1973	1,555	43	1,016	65	230	15	353	23
1974	3,401	122	2,672	79	341	10	510	15
1975	3,974	131	3,017	76	482	12	606	15
1976	5,243	139	4,140	79	591	11	651	12
1977	5,858	150	4,545	75	690	12	773	13
1978	7,017	208	5,359	77	902	13	935	13
1979	11,167	486	9,022	81	1,400	13	1,231	11
1980	13,403	100	11,057	82	1,236	9	1,209	9
1981	9,363	132	5,551	59	1,869	20	2,076	22

Note: a. Adjusted for imported service charges (i.e. minus sectoral totals equals GDP), which inflates sectoral relative shares.
Source: Ministry of Planning, *Annual Statistics 1981*.

negative growth rates during 1970–80.

Indicators of declining agricultural production and productivity are ample. In this context, we may note the following:

(1) The fact that the agricultural sector's relative share in GDP had declined more than the sector's share in the labour force no doubt offers an implicit indicator of emerging underemployment, and hence of declining productivity.
(2) The index number of leading agricultural products shows either stagnating or generally declining trends. This has been particularly so in recent years, where during 1978–80 the sector's index of production was 90 (based on 1969–81 = 100 index).[9]
(3) Thus the large rise in incomes, continued rural-urban migration and the presence of much imported labour, all created a huge supply gap in agricultural products. The natural outcome was increased imports of foodstuffs, thus deepening the dependency on the external sector. This is clearly demonstrated in Table 6.5, where during 1973–9, total agricultural imports increased by six times, and the sector's trade balance (i.e. export-import ratio) declined from 31 to 4 per cent, respectively.

The continuing deterioration of the agricultural sector, despite heavy investment and overall support, no doubt reflects persistent problems which severely curtail its growth. Briefly, these problems include inefficient management, the absence of a satisfactory agricultural structure, limited large-scale investment in developing physical, institutional and socio-economic infrastructure in rural areas, and continued soil salinity.

Table 6.5: Iraqi Agricultural Products: Exports and Imports, 1973–9 ($ million)

	Exports	Imports	Exports/Imports (per cent)
1973	7,625	24,604	31
1974	5,312	81,992	6
1975	5,833	90,510	6
1976	6,368	72,703	9
1977	5,983	91,029	7
1978	6,106	111,184	5
1979	6,535	148,548	4

Source: Arab Fund for Economic and Social Development (*et al.*), *Joint Arab Economic Report* (Kuwait, 1981), p. 201.

The Challenge of the War

The Extent of the Conflict

When the war started, Iraq was on the threshold of embarking on an intensive development drive. This was clearly exemplified by the five-year plan of 1981–5. The magnitude of the plan is revealed by the size of its total allocated expenditures of I.D. 40 billion ($135 billion at I.D. = $3.37), or I.D. 8 billion ($27 billion) per annum. Thus the first year of the plan coincided with the full impact of the war.

The impact of the war on the economy can best be appreciated by referring first to the salient features of the war itself. This can be briefly indicated as follows:

(1) *Intensity.* There is no doubt that the Iran-Iraq war finds no close equivalent in modern wars in terms of intensity of engagements. Indeed, it could easily be said that this war represents a state of virtual continuous battle.

(2) *Duration.* That the war has continued for two and a half years without let-up is in itself not only a demonstration of its uniqueness, but also of Iraq's ability to resist as well as to endure.

(3) *Character.* No doubt the war has virtually become a testing

ground for the most sophisticated kinds of modern weaponry. This fact has made it not only extremely expensive, but it has also exerted a tremendous pressure for matching the quality of human response. The war record so far shows here again that such pressures have been adequately met by Iraq.

(4) *Comparative forces.* Finally, all indicators point to the fact that Iraq was, and still is, fighting against many odds, particularly those relating to size, both of population and geographical area, whereas Iran possesses a much more extensive strategic depth.

Consequently, a war of this type must have heavily taxed Iraq's resources, both human and material, on an extensive scale. In doing so, it has generated intense interaction between continuing the war effort on the one hand and economic policy reaction on the other.

Development Pressures

Many symptoms of an over-heated economy were evident prior to the war. These were produced by the intensive development drive which began in earnest in 1974. In its earlier phase, the advent of the war had to a large extent aggravated existing pressures rather than generated some of its own. But as the war continued unabated, certain war-related problems started to emerge.

Such an intensive development drive was a direct result of the overall public sector expenditures in general, and the development programme in particular; and this relates to size, speed of implementation, composition and method of finance.

There is no doubt that the size of public expenditures and their high rate of implementation exerted great and continuous pressures on both domestic and absorptive capacities. Between 1976 and 1980, actual development expenditures increased by 3.4 times, from I.D. 935 million to I.D. 3,224 million. This was paralleled by the increase in current public sector expenditures, which rose from I.D. 1,269 million to I.D. 5,178 million between 1976 and 1981, an average annual rate of 42 per cent.

As regards the composition of development expenditures, because most of the large projects (in industry, agriculture and transportation) had long gestation periods, they generated large incomes without creating a corresponding supply of goods and services. This was aggravated by the fact that oil revenues were the main source of public expenditure financing. Unlike tax-financed expenditures, oil revenues only augment the income stream, they do not reduce it. Hence, they are essentially inflationary-biased.

There is no escaping the fact that all this demand pressure must show itself somewhere, and that it did so in a wide sense. It found its expression in many fields, including housing and building materials, land and real estate speculation, the labour market, money supply and prices.

As early as 1977, as the development drive gathers momentum, there was a sharp increase in the cost of building materials. This trend continued throughout early 1982, resulting in some cases in the emergence of black markets. Similarly, spot shortages in some consumer commodities resulted in a noticeable increase in their price. Experience shows, however, that the limitations of the distribution system had much to do with these shortages.

As regards the labour market, the same general trends were also present as the intensive development drive led both to overall shortages in labour and, consequently, to substantial increases in wages. Obviously, however, the increase in the cost structure was not only due to wage increases. Rising costs of imported commodities represent an important element in this respect.

On the other hand, since the mid-1970s Iraq had followed a very liberal policy on imported labour, particularly from the Arab countries. This factor, plus turn-key projects involving imported labour, did much to mitigate the impact of the continued demand for manpower for military purposes.

The obvious outcome of continued demand pressures was the substantial increase in both money supply and prices. Thus, during 1974–81, the average rate of increase in the former was about 35 per cent annually. As for prices, the annual rate of inflation for 1970–80 was 14.1 per cent, compared to only 1.7 per cent for 1960–70.[10] Moreover, the largest increase in prices was in food products, followed by the housing sector, despite the huge subsidies enjoyed by these products.

The Impact of the War

On the economic front, the most crucial impact of the war has been on the oil sector, where production was drastically reduced from 3.5 million b/d in 1980 (an eight-month average) to 838,000 b/d in

1982 a decline of 76 per cent. This has produced a chain reaction of effects which may be briefly noted:

(1) A dramatic decline in GDP in 1981 amounting to 50 per cent; the corresponding decline in GNP *per capita* was 33 per cent.

(2) The emergence of a large trade-balance deficit.

(3) A substantial decline in sulphur production and exports, due to the development of labour shortages as well as disruptions to the transportation system.

(4) Increased imports of fuel products and a corresponding increase in fuel costs.

(5) The emergence of a large budgetary deficit for 1981, amounting to over I.D. 1.5 billion. This, however, was amply covered by the large accumulated surpluses of previous years.

Economic Policy Reaction

In order to understand the nature and extent of economic policy reaction, it is imperative to examine it within the context of the most crucial element in the process of income determination in the Iraqi economy, namely, the external sector. The record since the war began demonstrates most vividly that the major thrust of economic policy has taken place in response to changes in this sector. For this sector constitutes both the 'engine of growth' as well as the 'safety valve' in the country's economy.

Export revenues, particularly from oil, represent the dynamic force in the development drive in that they provide its major source of finance. Rising revenues mean rising public expenditures, hence income, demand and consumption. Imports, on the other hand, denote the 'strategic' factor in the development process because of a number of functions performed. These include:

(1) Providing for real investment in the form of imported capital goods. This is the 'development' function.

(2) Making available a variety of consumer goods in response to rising incomes and standards of living. This is the 'social welfare' function.

(3) Providing a crucial investment for economic policy in its efforts to stabilize economic activity. By expanding the supply base it thus constitutes a major avenue for syphoning off inflationary pressures. This is the 'policy' function.

Thus, within the context of economic policy reaction to the changing situation in the external sector, we may distinguish three successive policy phrases, with the measures involved in each increasing in severity as the war continues with no end in sight.

Phase I: Beginning of The War to End 1981

During this period, confidence was high in Iraq's ability to wage a battle on the two fronts simultaneously: development and war. Consequently, most of the policy measures undertaken in this period were not only decided upon before the outbreak of hostilities, but some were actually being implemented even then. In short, these measures were essentially development- and not war-oriented.

Phase II: Throughout 1982

Early in 1982 a major decision was taken concerning the investment programme: that a 'pause' was needed in order to re-evaluate this programme. The outcome essentially revolved around the conviction that the size of public investment had already reached the level which was commensurate with the economy's absorptive capacity; what remained to be done should involve a thorough review of the scale of priorities, including the on-going development strategy.

Following this decision, a variety of policy measures were introduced. These can be briefly outlined as follows:

(1) Priorities in the investment programme included: repairing the war damage, and speeding up the implementation of projects already under way, as well as injecting specified measures of flexibility into the non-priority projects incorporated in the year's investment programme.

(2) A strict emphasis on financial guidelines in public expenditures.

(3) Stressing the rational use of foreign exchange resources. This applied to public, current and private spending, as well as the introduction of measures to encourage private savings.

(4) The implementation of major changes in the distribution network, aimed at reducing its severe bottlenecks.

(5) Introducing measures to reduce and/or overcome prevailing bottlenecks in public sector operations caused by bureaucratic routine.

(6) Enhancing the role of the private sector, particularly through

a more liberal imports policy as well as through measures to encourage private investment in industry.

(7) Implementing measures to improve the effectiveness of tax performance.

(8) Continuing the subsidy policy for basic necessities, as well as maintaining price support for a variety of consumer goods.

(9) Imposing a temporary halt to Iraq's foreign aid programme.

Phase III: Beginning with 1983

In this phase, which is still in effect, the foreign exchange consideration became the critical element; hence, most of the measures undertaken were geared at preserving and/or increasing the supply of these reserves. The severity of this element was further increased due to the conviction that the war would continue, hence Iraq had to prepare itself for the worst.

Consequently, the measures to be introduced included:

(1) Halting the implementation of 'non-essential' investment projects;

(2) reducing the scale of the imports programme through: (a) drastically reducing private imports; (b) effecting large reductions in public sector imports; and (c), as regards consumer goods imports, stressing only the necessities;

(3) halting foreign travel for other than extreme cases;

(4) introducing strong measures to encourage supply-based exports.

Implications and Prospects

Experience yields lessons; and the most severe of these lessons are learnt during periods of war. There is no doubt that the critical, most deeply absorbed lesson has been the realization that the Iraqi economy and its future development will continue suffering from their heavy dependence on foreign trade, but particularly oil revenues. This must change, however painful and difficult it may be, starting with the agricultural and industrial sectors.

The shift of priorities towards the development of the agricultural sector implies a recognition that all has not gone well in policy adopted in this sector. This emphasis stems from a number of considerations, which include the following:

(1) Agriculture is a sector which engages more than 50 per cent of the labour force.
(2) The actual performance of agriculture has fallen far short of its excellent potential.
(3) There is an increased worry of using food imports, hence the dangers of a 'food security' dimension and dependence on imports.
(4) The realization exists that achieving a 'green revolution' is indeed a prerequisite for building and sustaining an adequate industrial base, as well as a more over-all and balanced development.

The development of a broader industrial base is meant to be the major vehicle for reducing dependence on the oil sector. This industrial strategy includes:

(1) the diversification of industry outside the oil sector;
(2) emphasizing import-substitution strategy as a stage in establishing the desired industrial base;
(3) encouraging the role of the private sector through increased participation;
(4) paying special attention to increasing productivity and the efficiency of project execution and resource use in this sector.

As regards the interaction between the foreign sector and the development drive, particularly from the finance side, it is being increasingly realized that a 'qualitative' change of philosophy is much needed. This would involve softening, if not severely breaking, the direct link which has existed so far between oil export revenues and public spending. The availability of resources, and financial resources at that, may aid development but it may equally handicap development if not properly exploited.

Yet, despite all these obstacles, Iraq's development potential is undeniable. With huge oil reserves still untouched, a future source of development finance is thus readily available. And if the country's agricultural potential is realized, this source of 'permanent oil' can truly become the bread basket for all the Arab Gulf countries and beyond. Above all, efforts to eradicate illiteracy and raise the people's standard of health are bound to bear fruit in the future. It was this very potential which the war, imposed on Iraq, was meant to contain.

Wars cause damage and involve heavy sacrifices. The Iran-Iraq war has, no doubt, inflicted severe damage on Iraq in terms of loss of materials, destruction of vital installations, and loss of oil revenues, the major source of financing public sector expenditures. The rebuilding of all these will require substantial resources and effort.

Yet wars are transitory phenomena, or so we hope! And if the present conflict has brought any benefits at all, it has virtually forced the much-needed rethinking of priorities, created pressures for a more effective use of resources, and, above all, clearly demonstrated that time is of the essence and that it is indeed a crucial factor of production.

In the ultimate analysis, economic performance in times of an emergency cannot be judged by the availability of reasonably adequate resources; this is a gift of nature. More crucial is knowing what to do with them and having the will and capability to use them effectively, an attribute of genuine leadership. The record of the war period has effectively demonstrated that Iraq possesses both. This is indeed a source of inspiration: for he who can endure militarily so well can only succeed economically.

Notes

1. B. al-Bustany, 'Iraq: Economic Developments' in R. Erb (ed.), *The Arab Oil-Producing States of the Gulf* (AEI, Washington, DC, 1980), pp. 38–44.

2. United Nations/ECWA, *Survey of Economic and Social Developments of the ECWA Region* (1982), p. 55.

3. B. al-Bustany, 'The Arab Economy: A Statistical Comparison', *The Arab Economist* (Oct. 1979), pp. 5–35. (In Arabic).

4. World Bank, *World Development Report, 1982* (Washington, DC, 1982), p. 125.

5. Ibid.

6. ECWA, *Survey*, pp. 68 and 119.

7. *World Development Report, 1982*, p. 131.

8. Ibid., p. 113.

9. Ibid., p. 111.

10. Ibid.

7 THE ATTITUDES OF THE ARAB GOVERNMENTS TOWARDS THE GULF WAR

G. H. Jansen

The attitude of the Arab Governments towards the Gulf war was initially determined, not by their appreciation of the rights and wrongs of the Shatt al-Arab dispute, but by their varied bilateral relationships with Iraq. Any frank appraisal of these attitudes comes down to trying to find an answer to the question: why did the Arabs, with the one notable exception of Jordan, *not* support Iraq? Early in the war the Iraqis complained, with some justification, that they were fighting on behalf of all the Arabs, but this plea clearly did not carry conviction with Iraq's Arab brethren.

Yet there are two very powerful reasons why the Arabs should have backed Iraq: the motivations of racial and religious solidarity. The war clearly has a racial basis since it is a dispute between Semitic Arabs and Aryan Persians. And it has a religious basis in that it is a dispute between the followers of Islam and the followers of that 'other religion' called Shi'ism — a term fully justified in the writer's view since Shi'ism, although it emerged from the bosom of Islam, has added so much to the original doctrine that it has long since become a separate faith. At best the Shi'a might be described as non-Islamic Muslims — a position they share with the Javanese of Indonesia and the Alevis of Eastern Anatolian Turkey. The Sunnis, for their part, play down this difference in public, although they admit to it in private. The Shi'a, however, do not hide the theological separation between themselves and the Sunnis, and the regime in Tehran has proclaimed the war a conflict between righteous Shi'a and satanic Sunnis. In the context of the present confrontation it would be foolish to ignore this difference.

Despite all this, explicit Arab support for Iraq has not been forthcoming because the Iraqis made no less than five mistakes in their handling of the war and their explanation of it. Their five mistakes were as follows:

First, Iraq did not consult with the other Arab governments before launching its attack. It has been said that Saddam Hussein consulted with the Saudis during a visit he made to Riyadh about a

81

month before the war began. This is scarcely credible: not only is Saddam Hussein a secretive operator by nature but the disclosure would have amounted to a massive breach of security. More credible is the report that, when Saddam Hussein later complained to Prince Saud al-Faisal (the Saudi Foreign Minister) at the lack of Arab support, Faisal replied that Iraq should have told its Arab brothers what it was going to do and thus sought their support beforehand. (In point of fact they would never have agreed to Iraq launching the attack.)

Second, the Iraqis had failed to give adequate publicity to the extent of Shi'a subversion inside Iraq in the months preceding the war, fomented, financed and guided from Iran. This subversion had reached a dangerous, indeed intolerable, level. The Iraqi government *had* to act to bring it to an end. Whether their action should have taken the form of invading Iran is a moot point: perhaps it would have been wiser for Iraq to have first tried the tactic of counter-subversion inside Iran by stirring up the already dissident Kurds, Arabs and Baluchis. Be that as it may, it is at least plausible to argue that Iraq was not the aggressor in the Gulf war since the *casus belli* was not of its making: it was replying to a subversive attack already made on its own security by the Khomeini regime. But the good case Iraq had on this issue was not presented to the world at that time, nor even for some time after the war began. The most probable reason for this Iraqi publicity failure lies in the difficulty for a totalitarian regime in admitting that its subjects are susceptible to such a thing as subversion, and the reluctance of a regime operating under the banner of socialism to admit that, after all it has done for its people, there can still be sections of the citizenry who are dissatisfied. How could such disloyalty and such ingratitude exist?

Third, from the very start the Iraqis presented this as One Man's War. In the Iraqi media there was an incessant drumroll of propaganda based on endless repetition of the four words 'Saddam Hussein's new Qadisiya'.[1] The Arab reaction to this claim was to say, 'If this is your very own war, then victory will be to your personal credit and defeat will be your personal responsibility. Get on with it — on your own.' The Iraqi leader cannot have it both ways: he cannot say, 'This is my war . . . but help!'

Fourth, one reason why the other Arabs did not feel committed to or involved in the war was that the Iraqis themselves, from very early on, adopted a relaxed attitude towards it, both in its military and in its economic aspects. After their initial thrust into Iran and after they had partially surrounded the towns of Khuzistan, the Iraqi army sat down on its backside in siege positions, which they made very comfortable for themselves. For months on end there was no military action of any sort. Perhaps the soldiers were justified in taking it easy since on the home front the slogan was 'Business as usual'. In one sense it was a good thing that Iraq's development programme went ahead; but it was surely not a good thing, and very bad for fighting morale, that civilian life made no concessions to the fact that there was a war on. At one time the Iraqis even jeered at the Iranians because they had rationing and food queues. It would have been better for Iraq if it had itself adopted some visible measures of stringency. The Arab reaction to the Iraqi posture was: 'If you are taking your war easy, then so will we.' A war that is half fought is a war that will be fully lost.

Fifth, even on the purely legal issue of Iraqi rights to the Shatt al-Arab, the Iraqi authorities could not present their case to the Arabs, or to the rest of the world, on the broad basis of right and wrong. This was so because they had already conceded, by signing the 1975 Algiers Agreement with the Shah, that legal rights could be bent by superior strength. It all came down to a question of who would prevail on the battlefield, not who had the better legal case.

These tactical Iraqi errors notwithstanding, the general Arab criticism of Iraq's involvement in a war with Iran was that it distracted Arab attention and resources away from the main Arab problem of Palestine. This was genuinely felt by most ordinary Arabs, and certainly very strongly felt by the PLO — though it may be doubted whether many Arab governments were moved to serious displeasure with Iraq on this score.

We now come to the particular attitudes of individual Arab governments.

Jordan's motive for standing firmly and exceptionally by Iraq lay largely in the personal qualities of King Hussein. He is a plunger, and if he adopts a policy he follows it through with energy and enthusiasm. Having become friendly with Saddam Hussein, it was in his nature to stand by him in time of trouble. There are also solid economic reasons for the Jordanian stance. Over the years the economies of the two countries had become quite tightly inter-twined. Long before the war, the Jordanian port of Aqaba had become an important channel for Iraqi imports. Indeed, a part of the port was leased to Iraq for its exclusive use, and it made considerable funds available for the port's development and for road construction between Aqaba and Iraq. Iraq was conspicuously regular in the payment of its share of Arab funds allotted to Jordan by the 1978 Arab Summit; and there were several joint development projects on hand or envisaged, even including one for the diversion of the Euphrates water to north-eastern Jordan. Finally, as a monarch, King Hussein naturally disliked a regime that had put an end to another monarchical regime (the Shah's).

At the other end of the spectrum, in the group of Arabs who actively opposed Iraq and actively supported Iran, the key country was *Syria*. Its centrality followed from the fact it was an immediate neighbour of Iraq, while the other members of the Steadfastness and Confrontation Front were far away and could make little direct impact on the war. Why, however, should Hafez al-Assad's regime have backed non-Arab Iran against Arab Iraq? From very early on in the Iranian revolution, the Syrian leadership had shown sympathy for the Khomeini movement. The writer's suggestion is that this basic sympathy was due to the fact that the Shi'a in the Muslim world and the Alawites in Syria are both minorities facing a hostile Sunni majority: the Shi'a form only ten per cent of all Muslims and the Alawites only 16 per cent of the population of Syria. (The Alawites themselves, incidentally, claim to be Shi'a, although they are considered very heterodox even by the mainstream Shi'a of Iran: an examination of their beliefs suggests that they are really polytheistic pagans.) It has been said that the present antagonism between Syria and Iraq is merely the latest manifestation of the ancient enmity that has always opposed Damascus and Baghdad (comparable to the age-old rivalry between the rulers of the Valley of the Nile and those of the Valley of the Twin Rivers). But do these atavistic historical impulses really affect policy today? The theory at least needs close scrutiny by scholars. At all events, the form that Syrian/Iraqi antagonism has recently taken is rather that of rivalry between two wings of the Baath party, based in their respective capitals. It may, however, be doubted whether this furnishes a genuine cause for their antagonism, since there is precious little left of the original Baathist ideology in the governmental policies of either wing. In any case, how is one to understand Baathist ideology since it is expressed in the impenetrably obscure writings of Michel Aflaq? The only really 'ideological' difference between the two Baathist regimes is that, while in Syria it is the army that dominates the civilian element in the party, it is the other way around in Iraq.

South Yemen: For many years the Iraqi Baath party had close connections with and many supporters in North Yemen. Accordingly, when the two Yemens fell out, Iraq was ill-disposed to the South; and when the Gulf war started, South Yemen returned the compliment. Another probable reason for South Yemen's attitude is that Soviet influence is stronger there than in any other Arab country; and the Russians, despite a treaty of friendship, do not like the Iraqi regime for having tricked Iraq's communists into supporting the regime and then excluded them from any effective share in power.

Libya: One has no less difficulty in penetrating Ghaddafi's motives for opposing Iraq in the Gulf war than in understanding anything else that the Colonel does. For many years Libya has considered Iraq to be a non-militant back-slider from the Steadfastness and Confrontation Front. It may be recalled that, when this Front was formally constituted at a meeting in Tripoli soon after Camp David, Iraq attended but then walked out, declaring that the Front had no positive alternative to the Camp David plan. Also we may surmise that Libya was attracted by the radical, dynamic aspects of the Iranian revolution — which was both anti-monarchical and strongly anti-American; and this Libyan-Iranian fellow-feeling survived Iran's anger with the Libyan regime for having caused the disappearance of the Lebanese Shi'a leader, Imam Mousa Sadr. Although the Lebanese Shi'a have not forgotten or forgiven, Khomeini's regime evidently found it convenient to do so.

Algeria: In the light of Algeria's geographical remoteness, its opposition to Iraq may perhaps have been based on the general principle that Iraq's involvement in a war with Iran had caused a distraction from Palestine and was wasting Arab resources on a side issue. But Algeria had a bilateral grudge too against Iraq for not supporting the Polisario movement which it was backing itself. In point of fact, Iraq simply could not advocate self-determination for the Polisario without conceding the same right to sections of its own populace, such as the Kurds and Shi'a.

There were thus four Arab countries openly opposed to Iraq while only one (Jordan) openly espoused its cause. But there were other Arab countries that gave Iraq oblique and covert support. From *Tunisia* and *Morocco* Iraq received verbal sympathy. These conservative regimes had never approved of Iraq's radical socialism but did not actively oppose it because they were not actively threatened by it. On the other hand, they actively disliked the Khomeini regime in view of the disturbing influence of its ideas on Muslim opposition movements in their own two countries.

Amongst other Arab countries giving active but discreet support was Egypt, which provided military assistance. Sadat himself was quite open in his sympathy for the Shah, because, after all, they were rulers of the same basic kind — absolute, personal, grandiloquent, and with a passion for gaudy uniforms. More positively and to his credit, Sadat also felt gratitude (that very rare quality in politics) towards the Shah for having supplied Egypt with oil when it badly needed it during the 1973 war. Also Iraq's purchases of Russian arms from Egypt were paid for in hard currency, and this was a useful contribution to the Egyptian budget. (Russian weapons were in any case no longer needed by Egypt, which was switching to American models.)

Active but discreet support for Iraq came also from *Saudi Arabia* and the *Gulf states* in terms of financial and logistical backing. The attitude of these states towards the Gulf war, having as they did reason to fear both Iraq and Iran, was something of a balancing act. On the one hand, they had all felt threatened by the ideological subversion which Iraq had tried to export earlier on; and there was Iraq's territorial claim to Kuwait. On the other hand, they were no less fearful of Iranian imperial expansion, taken over as it had been by Khomeini's regime. The latter had revived the Iranian claim on Bahrain, vindicated the Shah's seizure of the islands in the lower Gulf, and bombed oil installations near Kuwait. Moreover, all these states, though dominated by Sunnis, have Shi'a minorities and were alarmed at the prospect of increased disaffection amongst them instigated by Khomeini. For all these reasons, it was not surprisingly alleged that Saudi Arabia and the Gulf states were not averse to an indefinite prolongation of the war so that both sides would be weakened. Recognizing, however, that Iraq was Arab and judging it the lesser threat of the two, this group of states afforded Iraq much covert assistance. Their outright financial grants are thought to have reached (at the time of writing) between $20 and $27 billion; and they opened their ports and lines of communication for traffic to and from Iraq after the closure of Basra.

If the war proves likely to drag on indefinitely, or if the likelihood of outright Iranian victory is seen as growing, there may well be modifications in the attitudes of all these Arab countries. Those which initially viewed the possible humiliation of Iraq with favour, no less than those disposed, reluctantly or not, to give Iraq discreet support, may well see that a prolongation of the war is so damaging to everyone's interests (including their own) that the pursuit of an armistice overrides all other considerations and that each and all should do what they can to persuade the combatants to call off the fighting.

Note

1. In AD 636, the Persian Sassanids were defeated at the Battle of Qadisiya, near Hira, by the Arab armies of General Sa'd bin Abi Waqqas.

8 THE ATTITUDES OF THE SUPERPOWERS TOWARDS THE GULF WAR*

M. S. El Azhary

For almost three years now the United States and the Soviet Union have found themselves sitting on the sidelines of the war between Iraq and Iran. It is this lack of leverage to influence the course of the war that best characterizes, and to a very large extent, as I will show in the following pages, has shaped the attitudes of the superpowers towards the conflict. In analysing these attitudes one cannot exclude from the discussion such wider issues as American and Soviet interests in the Gulf and the Middle East as a whole. One has to take into consideration the bilateral relations between the superpowers and particular regimes in the area, such as the US 'special' relationship with Saudi Arabia and Oman, or regional factors such as inter-Arab politics, the Soviet intervention in Afghanistan, and the Arab-Israeli conflict. Nonetheless, at the risk of over-simplifying matters, attention will be centred on the relations of the United States and the Soviet Union with both Iraq and Iran and the impact of these relations on the course of the fighting. This will be done in the context of the superpowers' stakes in the war, their military and diplomatic actions in attempting to influence the course (and the outcome) of the conflict, and their gains and losses in terms of influence with the combatants and in the region in general.

The Carter Administration

When the Gulf war broke out on 22 September, 1980, it created difficulties and potential dangers for the US which remain very real. Those difficulties and dangers basically stem from the over-riding strategic reality the 60 per cent of the world's oil trade comes from the Gulf region. With the Iranian and Iraqi shipments already

*This article also appeared in *International Affairs* (London), vol. 59, no. 4 (Autumn 1983). Reprinted by permission.

disrupted, the Carter administration feared that a spread of violence in the region might result in a severe petroleum shortage that would undermine Western economic strength and political cohesion. Former President Carter underscored this concern when he declared that, while the West was in a position to cope with an interruption of Iranian and Iraqi supplies, it was nevertheless 'imperative that there be no infringement' of the ability of other suppliers to ship oil out of the Gulf.[1]

While substantial Western interests were involved, however, the Carter administration was virtually powerless to influence the course of the fighting on the Shatt al-Arab. Consequently it adopted a neutral posture. Direct military intervention by the Carter administration was thereby ruled out, and only in the event of an attempted Iranian blockade of the Strait of Hormuz would American warships and aircraft have been called upon. The US already had a naval task force in place nearby in the Arabian Sea since the Soviet intervention in Afghanistan a year earlier.[2] As is so often the case in the Middle East, however, where events seem to shape decisions rather than the reverse, within twenty-four hours of the Carter administration's declaration of neutrality, the leaders of Saudi Arabia requested US military assistance against possible Iranian attack.

The Carter administration's response was to send four AWACS (Airborne Warning and Control Systems) reconnaissance planes with their ground support systems to the Kingdom, as had been done once before, in March 1979 during the border war between North and South Yemen. In this instance, it proved the ideal means for the US to demonstrate its concern for the security of Saudi Arabia without provoking the Soviet Union by introducing new 'offensive' military systems.[3]

The dispatch of the AWACS was considered consistent with the 'Carter Doctrine' that the US was prepared to use military force to protect Gulf oil supplies from external threats. By responding to Saudi Arabia in this way, however, the Carter administration seems to have expanded US commitment further. It raised the possibility of introducing American military power into internal regional conflicts in order to ensure a continued flow of oil. Moreover, the US, inspired by Saudi Arabia's request for military protection, embarked on a military co-operative effort with its Western allies to increase their collective naval presence in the Arabian Sea and the Indian Ocean area. In less than three weeks, the number of allied warships was increased from 30 to 60, including warships from France, Britain and Australia, as well as from the US.[4] This action was taken in great haste in the belief that, following the dispatch of AWACS to Saudi Arabia, an action on a multi-national basis was likely to be more politically acceptable to the Gulf states than unilateral American action.

In contrast to the publicity that accompanied the dispatch of the AWACS — intended perhaps as a psychological deterrent to Iran — the increase in allied naval presence in the area was executed with minimum publicity. There were no formal declarations or high visibility crisis management meetings between the allies, who apparently were trying to avoid the appearance of overreaction to the Gulf war crisis and, at the same time, trying to avoid needless provocation of the Soviet Union. In the meantime, the US hurriedly launched an effort to strengthen its quick-reaction force, the Rapid Deployment Force (RDF), still then in its early stages of development.

During the early weeks of the war, from the standpoint of the US, the worst did not occur; indeed, as a by-product, the crisis may have even strengthened America's defence posture in the region. By the positioning of more planes and ships within striking distance of the fighting, the Carter administration was able to exercise a deterrent effect against a widening of the war. It was thought at the time that Iraq was planning to launch attacks against Iran from Oman and Saudi Arabia;[5] if this was the case, the Carter administration was in a position to discourage those two countries from becoming militarily involved, and so to contain the conflict. At the same time, it reminded Iran and Iraq that the US was determined to prevent the war between them from shutting off the flow of oil to the rest of the world.

To express their appreciation of the Western stand, the Saudis reciprocated by prompt action of their own to ease the strain on oil supplies caused by the war. A few days after dispatch of the AWACS, Saudi Arabia decided to increase its oil production and organized similar efforts with such other major producers as Kuwait and the United Arab Emirates. This action had the effect of insulating the international petroleum market against the effects of the war.[6] It should be pointed out, however, that previous to the Saudi decision to raise oil production, the Carter administration had succeeded in reducing somewhat the sense of crisis by announcing that 'oil inventories of the world's major oil-consuming nations were at an all-time high'.[7]

By requesting American military assistance and supporting the US effort to strengthen its military presence in the area, the Saudi leaders appeared less wary of such direct military collaboration than in the past. Although the Carter administration, at this early stage, did not focus directly on the long-term strategy for building up American forces in the Gulf area, the crisis was seen by the American side as a crucial first step in closer military co-operation with Saudi Arabia in the future. Commenting with satisfaction on the US-Saudi military collaboration, a Carter administration official was quoted as contending that the US was 'in a much better position to move ahead on building a security framework in South-West Asia'.[8] Nevertheless, once it seemed that the war would not spill over into the neighbouring countries, and the US had achieved its immediate objective of maintaining the flow of oil out of the Gulf region, administration policy was expressed in words rather than deeds, reflecting its lack of leverage with the combatants.

The Carter administration was concerned that the Soviet Union had much more diplomatic latitude in the crisis than the US. Not only did Moscow have functioning relations with both belligerents, but it had also been the principal military supplier of the Iraqis. It was, therefore, in a position to reap diplomatic advantages. One fear was that, as in the 1971 war between India and Pakistan, Moscow might offer itself as a mediator in peace talks between Tehran and Baghdad. Should that happen, Moscow might also acquire new political influence in the region as a whole — a development the US had long sought to prevent.

With this in mind, former US Secretary of State Edmund Muskie enunciated two key 'principles' in a proposal to end the Gulf war:

> We believe this conflict can and must be resolved through respect for international law — that territory must not be seized by force of arms, that disputes should be resolved by practical means.
>
> And let us also affirm another principle that will be essential to a peaceful resolution of this conflict. It is the principle that neither side should seek to interfere in the affairs of the other.[9]

The first point was directed at Iraq which, as noted below, had aroused concern in Washington by what was seen as an effort to separate the oil-producing province of Khuzistan from the rest of

Iran. The point concerning non-interference referred to Iran. Iraq's complaint that Iran was attempting to export its brand of revolution to the Shi'a Muslim population of Iraq was considered by the Carter administration to be valid. More important, perhaps, is that by stating these principles, the Carter administration was trying to prevent any intervention by the Soviet Union.

Another cause of anxiety to the Carter administration was the possibility of a definitive Iraqi victory which would result in what former President Carter called the 'dismemberment' of Iran. In expressing this concern, Carter said that the Iraqi forces had exceeded the war goal, which was to take control of the Shatt al-Arab waterway and 'no Iranian territory. . . . The carving out of a part of Iran to be separated from the rest would not be in our interest.'[10] It was thought that, in such an eventuality, Iran would be plunged into a civil war and the Soviet Union would intervene, either directly or indirectly. With these prospects in mind, the Carter administration was increasingly tempted to abandon strict neutrality and supply Iran with the desperately needed spare parts to operate its American-made military equipment. There were those among Carter's advisers (including Zbigniew Brzezinski) who argued that, since Iraq was receiving spare parts for its Soviet-made equipment, the US should correct the imbalance by supplying the needed spare parts to Iran. Such action hopefully would prevent the collapse of Iran. They believed the Khomeini regime to be anti-Soviet as well as anti-American.[11]

In addition, as it was then a presidential election season in the US, Carter administration officials perceived that the Iranian leaders considered the American election campaign to be a factor in setting the conditions for releasing the hostages held at the American embassy in Tehran. An offer of spare parts, therefore, in exchange for the hostages' release proved a very tempting means of enhancing Carter's chances of re-election. 'If the hostages are released safely we would make delivery of those items which Iran owns — which they have bought and paid for.' The former President was referring to an estimated $240 million in military equipment already purchased but not received by Iran, and which was frozen with Iran's other assets when the hostages were seized. The US would maintain its neutrality by refraining to sell 'additional' military equipment to Iran.[12]

The terms of the agreement that finally led to the hostages' release did not include a specific mention of military spare parts.

Despite the fluctuations in the progress of the negotiations over the hostages, the Iranians clearly wanted to reach an agreement before having to deal with the Reagan administration. In the event, the hostages were being freed as President Reagan's inauguration was in progress. At that point, the Gulf war had reached a stalemate and Iran appeared to be in less danger than at an earlier stage.

The Reagan Administration

The Reagan administration maintained the neutral stance and followed the policies towards Iraq and Iran established by the preceding administration. It continued to strengthen US presence in the area by concluding an access agreement to use air and naval facilities in Pakistan.[13] (With its coast on the Arabian Sea, Pakistan is considered an integral part of the Gulf region.) Strides were also made in building up Rapid Deployment Force (RDF) military units which became operational, as demonstrated in the US-organized military exercises which took place in several Arab and African countries (including Oman) in 1981 and 1982.

All of this seemed to advance further US capabilities for military intervention in the Gulf. Moreover, the Reagan administration cemented US-Saudi military co-operation by selling Saudi Arabia the AWACS thus reassuring the Saudi leaders that the US administration, despite its closeness to Israel, was firmly committed to continuing a policy of supporting Saudi Arabia and defending the Gulf region.

With regard to Iran, however, the Reagan administration tried to put some distance between itself and the former administration by an indirect rebuke for making the hostages deal. They would not have negotiated with the Iranians to obtain their release, they said.[14] The Carter administration's earlier promise of $240 million in military spare parts was cancelled. According to former Secretary of State Alexander Haig, there would be 'no military equipment provided to the government of Iran either under earlier obligations and contractual arrangements [or under] as yet unstated requests'.[15] Iran continued to request military spare parts from the US, however, particularly for the 80 American-built F-14 fighter planes inherited from the time of the late Shah. The last such request was made in December 1981. On that occasion, as on all others, the Reagan administration held fast to its policy of prohibiting the export of military equipment and high technology items to Iran.[16]

In contrast to this stern attitude towards Iran, the Reagan administration wanted to improve relations with Iraq. Early in 1981, in explaining the Reagan administration's plan to develop a 'strategic consensus' to counter Soviet expansionism, Haig held out the possibility of improved US-Iraqi relations. Washington, he said, had noted 'some shift' in Iraqi policy, caused in part by 'a greater sense of concern about the behavior of Soviet imperialism in the Middle Eastern area'.[17] Haig was referring to what the US viewed as a pattern of change in Iraqi diplomacy from a radical to a more moderate stance. That change encompassed close ties with Jordan, a *rapprochement* with Saudi Arabia, and a decline in Soviet-Iraqi relations. Those relations will be discussed further below.

More important, perhaps, the US was, and remains, hopeful (barring, of course, a change of regime under the present circumstances) that Iraq might take a more favourable view of the US role in Gulf security and a centrist position on the Arab-Israeli conflict. The Reagan administration has consistently refused to sell arms to Iran and has pursued its policy of remaining neutral in the Gulf war. Indeed, in recent years, the situation seemed so ripe for the above-mentioned shift by Iraq that one analyst was prompted to call it 'the West's opportunity'.[18]

US-Iraqi relations continued to improve despite the bombing by the Israelis of a nuclear reactor near Baghdad in June 1981. The Reagan administration condemned the Israeli attack and censured Israel in a United Nations Security Council vote. The text of the resolution was agreed upon by both the US and Iraq and was considered the harshest censure of Israel ever endorsed by the US at the UN.[19] The stage was then set for further progress in relations between the two countries.

On several occasions over the past three years President Saddam Hussein has expressed his interest in expanding diplomatic contacts with the US.[20] The Reagan administration has responded in kind. Iraq has been removed from the list of countries accused of aiding and abetting terrorism, thus lifting US restrictions against exports to Iraq.[21] US trade with Iraq is estimated at $1 billion a year, and although the US does not supply arms to Iraq, it has consistently supported France's policy of supplying military equipment to that country, which has now grown to constitute one third of Iraq's needs. The remainder comes from the Soviet Union, a point to be discussed further below.

As already noted, all of Iran's numerous requests for military equipment and spare parts have been rejected out of hand by the Reagan administration. To circumvent this embargo, Iran has turned to a number of countries in Eastern and Western Europe as well as to Israel, Syria, Libya and North Korea. One estimate puts the figure at between $100 and $200 million in arms, spare parts and ammunition delivered to Iran from Western Europe in the first eighteen months of the war. Approximately half this amount was supplied or arranged by Israel, the remainder by dealers on the international market, some of whom also may have connections with the Israelis. This diversity of arms sources is not new for Iran: Iran under the Shah had already begun to diversify its suppliers by purchasing arms from the Soviet Union.[22] Judging by the size of the Iranian armed forces, however, Iran could not have sustained its war effort, much less turn the tide against the Iraqis, by depending on the international arms market. It seems likely that Iran solved its military spare parts problem by discovering its own stock. Apparently the Iranian armed forces, after a chaotic year or more of combat, gradually managed to 'put their house in order' and used the massive amounts of ammunition and spare parts stockpiled during the time of the Shah. In the view of several observers, it was this solution to the spare parts problem, and not Islamic fervour, which broke the long deadlock in the war and routed the entrenched Iraqi troops from Iranian territory.[23]

Another reason for Iran's reversal of fortunes in the war was that, since the beginning of 1982, revolutionary turmoil had subsided within its borders and a gradual cohesion began to evolve. This came as a welcome development for the US because, with a pro-Soviet regime next door to Iran in Afghanistan, a strong anti-communist Iran was considered an important barrier to the extension of Soviet influence in the Gulf region. But Iran's revolutionary zeal has continued, and, as before, this has been viewed with alarm by its more conservative Arab neighbours as destabilizing for their regimes. Moreover, the Reagan administration has been under pressure from Saudi Arabia, the Gulf states and Jordan to shore up Iraq's resistance to Iran. In response, the administration has reiterated the US commitment to its friends in the area. In a comprehensive speech outlining the administration's Middle East policy, Alexander Haig affirmed US neutrality and added:

Neutrality, however, does not mean that we are indifferent to the outcome. We have friends and interests that are endangered by the continuation of hostilities. We are committed to defending our vital interests in the area. These interests and the interests of the world are served by the territorial integrity and political independence of all countries in the Persian Gulf.[24]

This declaration was accompanied by an announcement by Haig that the US would become more active in seeking a peaceful solution to the Gulf war. Although it is unlikely that the present Iranian regime would accept a peace initiative emanating either directly or indirectly from Washington, Haig's statement seemed to signal to Iran that the US wished better relations with that country in the future.

With regard to Iraq, just before Haig's statement, the Reagan administration disclosed that it had been in contact with Islamic mediating states with the aim of preventing Iranian forces from pushing ahead into Iraq (a further demonstration of the US's lack of leverage with the combatants).[25] Iran paid no heed to advice, and invaded Iraq in July 1982, with the objective not only of bringing down the government of Saddam Hussein but also of establishing an Islamic Republic in Iraq, and ultimately spreading the Islamic revolution to the other Gulf states. But the Iranian invasion failed, and again the war reached a stalemate. Since then Iraq has successfully repulsed several other offensives and for the time being the US's worst fears have not been realized.

The Soviet Union

The Soviet Union, like the US, was caught unawares when the Gulf war broke out, despite its close military ties with Iraq. Unlike the US, however, the Soviet Union is not threatened by the loss of access to Gulf oil because it is energy self-sufficient. However, the war found the Soviets in a mass of cross-currents regarding their own interests and vulnerabilities. They saw this as a war between two neighbouring states which maintain important, multi-faceted relations with the USSR. On the one hand, Iraq is an official ally linked to Moscow since 1972 by a treaty of friendship and co-operation; on the other, the anti-Americanism of the revolutionary regime in Iran had brought important gains for the Soviet Union.

At the same time, the USSR had been embroiled in a guerrilla war in Afghanistan, adding to what the Soviet leaders must have perceived as chaos along their southern reaches.

Very early in the war, Andrei Gromyko, the Soviet Foreign Minister, affirmed the neutral posture of the Soviet government.[26] Then followed President Leonid Brezhnev's call for Baghdad and Tehran to go to the negotiating table. He warned that the war might provide an excuse for the US to move into Iran militarily and control the Gulf oil under a pretext of freeing the American hostages.[27] The Soviet media also condemned the Carter administration for sending AWACS planes to Saudi Arabia, and increasing its western naval task force in the Arabian Sea and the Indian Ocean. Not mentioned, however, was the presence of the Soviet fleet, including 12 combat vessels and 17 support ships in the area.[28]

In order to counterbalance the growing military presence of the US, and reflecting Soviet concern about the growing acceptability of that presence (caused in part by the Gulf war), Brezhnev invited the US and other world powers to join the Soviet Union in a formal pact to forswear military intervention in the Gulf, and to guarantee the flow of oil to the rest of the world. On 23 February 1981 the Soviet leader repeated the proposal to the newly elected Reagan administration.[29]

With regard to the combatants in the Gulf war, the Soviet Union maintained an attitude of aloofness towards Iraq. In a joint communiqué issued in October 1980 at the end of talks between Brezhnev and the Syrian President Hafez al-Assad in Moscow, there was no mention of the Gulf war, which was in its second week. Instead, there was praise for the Iranian revolution. The communiqué made a clear attempt to restrain Iraq by declaring that Moscow and Damascus 'support the inalienable right of Iran to decide its destiny independently without any interference from outside'.[30]

Perhaps this was not totally unexpected because Soviet-Iraqi relations had been strained since the late 1970s. The Soviet leaders were particularly vexed when, in 1978, the Iraqi government ordered the execution of 21 communists for attempting to subvert the army. In spite of the intervention of the Soviet Union, Bulgaria, and East Germany on behalf of the doomed Communists, the executions proceeded. Iraq then reduced the number of Iraqis to receive military training in the Soviet Union as an expression of their concern about Marxist indoctrination. There have also on occasions been disagreements concerning economic and military co-operation, as Baghdad began to look more and more to the West for trade, technology and military equipment.[31]

Another indication of further deterioration in Soviet-Iraqi relations came during the Twenty-Sixth CPSU Congress in February 1981, when the head of the Iraqi communist party, Aziz Muhammad — presumably with the Kremlin's approval — condemned the war against Iran and demanded the immediate withdrawal of Iraqi troops from Iran. In contrast to the previous congress in 1976, the Iraqi Baath party did not send representatives.[32]

In contrast to these uneasy relations with Iraq, the Soviet leaders and the press, on numerous occasions, expressed their support for the revolution in Iran. In his report to the Twenty-Sixth CPSU Congress, President Brezhnev seemed far more cordial to Iran than to Iraq, praising the Iranian revolution as 'a major event on the international scene in recent years [which] is of a specific nature. However complex and contradictory, it is essentially an anti-imperialist revolution, though reaction at home and abroad is seeking to change this feature'. Brezhnev wished the Iranians success in their revolution and offered to 'develop good relations with Iran on the principles of equality and reciprocity'.[33] Brezhnev's words also seem to reflect the fact that the Soviet leadership was no longer apprehensive, at least in the short term, about the power of example of Iran's Islamic revolution and its possible effects in inspiring religious revivalism or disaffection among the Muslim population in the Central Asian republics of the USSR.

Up to this point, the Gulf war and the hostages crisis overlapped and Iran was in almost total isolation from the West. Under these circumstances, the Soviet leaders hoped that this would induce Iran to turn to them for help. The Soviet leadership also believed that, with the release of the American hostages, the US and Iran might move towards a *rapprochement*, particularly in view of Iran's need for military spare parts to continue its war with Iraq. To forestall such an eventuality, Moscow was prepared to supply Iran with Soviet arms, but evidently Iran rejected the offer.[34]

Despite these efforts to 'court' Iran, Moscow was unable to capitalize on the tightly strained US-Iranian relations and was making no headway in improving its own position in Iran. There were occasions on which the Iranian Islamic rulers vowed to view the US and the Soviet Union with an equally critical eye as long as Moscow refused to abandon its neutral position in the Gulf war in the face of 'flagrant Iraqi aggression against Iran', such was the message conveyed by the late Iranian Prime Minister, Muhammad Ali Rajai to Soviet ambassador Vladimir Vinogradov and made public by the Iranian government. Another matter of contention mentioned by Rajai was the Soviet intervention in Afghanistan, in spite of the Soviets' efforts to link the CIA with resistance movements in both Iran and Afghanistan.[35] Soviet broadcasts making this assertion were repeated throughout 1981.[36]

The Iranian demand for renegotiation of the price of natural gas shipped to the Soviet Union through the Iranian Natural Gas Trunkline (IGAT) is a further unresolved issue between the two countries. Even before the Gulf war, the flow of Iranian natural gas dropped off as a result of a decrease in oil production. There was a complete cut-off in March 1980, when Moscow rejected Iranian demands for a five-fold increase to bring the price up to world market levels.[37]

The Soviet Union's unrewarded 'courtship' of Iran was clearly causing frustration in the Kremlin which complained about a number of Iranian policies, including frequent anti-Soviet comments by Iranian leaders. In March 1982 *Pravda* expressed its displeasure with Iran in a commentary on the status of Soviet-Iranian relations. In less than enthusiastic terms, it noted that Soviet trade with Iran amounted to R800 million compared with R700 million in 1978, the last year of the Shah's reign. *Pravda* rated it as 'not bad'. It complained, however, that 'unfortunately such a claim cannot be made about other areas of Soviet-Iranian relations, which have been harmed in the past two or three years'. *Pravda* listed the reduction in Soviet diplomatic presence in Tehran, the closing of the Soviet consulate in Rasht, the closing of the Soviet-Iranian Cultural Relations Society, the closing of the Iran-Soviet Bank, the ban on Soviet reporters, and the closing of several other joint enterprises, as examples.

Pravda was particularly vexed that Iran had continued to speak of the USSR as one of 'two threats' — that from the north. (That from the south was the US.) The paper said that, 'equating Soviet and US policies only adversely portrays the policies of our nation and ignores the reality of international events'. It reminded Iran that the Soviet Union had granted Iran transit rights through Soviet territory after the US had ordered a blockade of the alternative route through the Gulf during the hostage crisis. Although the blockade was no longer in force, the Soviet Union had extended these rights to Iran during its war with Iraq. It is, perhaps, worth noting that this commentary by *Pravda*, like all other Soviet press and broadcast commentaries, avoided criticism of Ayatollah Khomeini and suggested instead that Iranian anti-Soviet attitudes were encouraged by 'right-wing' groups. The idea to be conveyed here is that those groups create 'obstacles to the expansion of Soviet-Iranian relations' and are harmful to 'the Iranian economy and Iran's ability to fight imperialist pressures'.[38]

Furthermore, since the Islamic revolution seized power in Iran, the Khomeini regime had held the communist Tudeh party on a short leash — tolerating it, yet preventing it from increasing its membership and influence. The party has remained under suspicion, as indicated by Prime Minister Hussein Moussavi's declaration that Tudeh members would face execution if, upon joining the Revolutionary Guards or other of the regime's organizations, they failed to state their party affiliation. This uneasy liaison came to an end in February 1983 when about 70 Tudeh members were arrested and accused of spying for the Russians. Two months later the Iranian government announced the dissolution of the Tudeh party, and on the same day ordered eight Soviet diplomats to leave the country. Although exasperated, no doubt, the Soviets have so far reacted relatively mildly by confining themselves to protesting at the expulsion of the diplomats.[39]

In light of the Soviet failure to establish closer links with Iran, Moscow has also kept its options open towards Iraq and decided early on to repair its deteriorating relations with Baghdad in the hope of preserving influence in the Iraqi capital after the war, as well as keeping intact the friendship treaty between the two countries.

In April 1981, a little more than a month after the Twenty-Sixth CPSU Congress, the Soviet Union and Iraq celebrated the ninth anniversary of their treaty as though nothing had changed. An Iraqi delegation visited Moscow for the occasion, and the Iraqi President, Saddam Hussein, and his Soviet counterpart, Leonid Brezhnev, exchanged messages expressing their desire to strengthen ties 'based on mutual co-operation'. Brezhnev stated, 'We are convinced that the treaty can serve well the basic interests of the people of the Soviet Union and Iraq in the struggle against imperialist intrigues and form a just and durable peace in the

Middle East.'[40] For its part, Iraq found it agreeable to continue the treaty with the Soviet Union, largely because Iraq has been obtaining Soviet-made weapons and spare parts from Eastern Europe. It is highly unlikely that the Soviet Union's allies would provide such arms without prior Soviet approval. According to Iraqi Deputy Premier Tariq Aziz, this indirect solution for providing arms to Iraq helped Iraq and the Soviet Union avoid a major impasse. 'If we had failed [to get Soviet arms] we might have become irritated, very hostile, very hysterical against the Soviet Union,' which, he said, would have been a mistake. Aziz added, 'Now we can behave serenely with the Soviet Union without being hostile to them'.[41]

About two-thirds of Iraq's military equipment is Soviet-made (down from 95 per cent in 1972 when the treaty was signed); the remainder comes from France and, to a lesser extent, Britain and Italy. Iraq has signed contracts with both Eastern and Western European countries for military equipment amounting to billions of dollars since the start of the war.[42]

The Soviet Union is continuing its indirect flow of military supplies to the Iraqi armed forces and has given valuable assistance to Iraq in the repair of war-damaged, Soviet-built industrial plants. In addition, the two countries have signed a number of commercial and technological agreements, but not on a scale that exceeds that of the 1972 agreement. Much of Iraq's trade now is with Japan, West Germany, France and the US. In 1980 the Soviet Union ranked 14th among Iraq's trade partners. There is a strong possibility, however, that, in a post-war reconstruction effort, Soviet-Iraqi economic ties will be strengthened considerably.[43]

At all events, the Soviet Union seems to have been able to maintain its links with Iraq, while simultaneously trying to 'court' Iran and thereby straddle the dispute. Lacking leverage with both combatants, the USSR has succeeded, by the use of caution and restraint, in avoiding irreparable damage to its relations with either side. Whether or not the Soviet Union will be able to continue this policy will depend upon what Iraq and Iran achieve on the battle-field. As already noted, Iraq has so far succeeded in repulsing Iranian attacks on its territory, and the two sides appear locked in an inconclusive war.[44] Since the situation on the battlefield has reverted to a stalemate, as in most of the last three years, the Soviet Union has no choice but to continue its policy of courting both countries in order to prevent a total shift by either one to the United

States. But should Iraq suffer a severe and definitive defeat and the Baathist regime of President Saddam Hussein be overthrown and replaced by a pro-Khomeini regime, with all that would imply in terms of incalculable ramifications for the rest of the Gulf region and the entire Middle East, that eventuality would not necessarily serve the interests of the Soviet Union. It would, however, bring important gains for the USSR — at least in terms of the anti-American and anti-Western actions which would probably damage existing Western interests and relations in the region.

Notes

1. *New York Times*, 25 Sept. 1980.
2. The US naval task force included a total of 18 combat ships and 13 support ships headed by the aircraft-carriers *Midway* and *Eisenhower*. Both can launch about 170 aircraft. France also had a task force consisting of 14 vessels, as part of the West's presence in the area. *Washington Post*, 3 Oct. 1980.
3. *New York Times*, 30 Sept. 1980.
4. *Washington Post*, 20 Oct. 1980.
5. *New York Times*, 12 Oct. 1980.
6. Ibid., 4 Oct. 1980.
7. Ibid., 25 Sept. 1980. The United States' oil reserves were estimated at 100 days. *Washington Post*, 28 Sept. 1980.
8. *New York Times*, 12 Oct. 1980.
9. Ibid., 21 Oct. 1980.
10. Ibid., 19 Oct. 1980.
11. Ibid., 22 Oct. 1980.
12. *Washington Post*, 29 Oct. 1980.
13. The use of the Pakistani naval base at Gwandar and the air base at Peshewar. *New York Times*, 5 March 1981.
14. Ibid., 19 Feb. 1981. During the 1980 presidential campaign, however, candidate Ronald Reagan supported the negotiations based on Ayatollah Khomeini's four points and did not criticize the Carter administration's tactics once the negotiations had begun.

15. Haig also urged American companies to exercise 'careful caution' before resuming trade with Iran. *Washington Post*, 29 Jan. 1981.

16. *New York Times*, 13 Dec. 1981.

17. Ibid., 20 March 1981. Haig followed this by sending Deputy Assistant Secretary of State Morris Draper to Baghdad to brief Iraq on Haig's tour of other Middle East capitals and to clarify the Reagan administration's views on the region.

18. See Adeed Dawisha, 'Iraq: the West's Opportunity', *Foreign Policy*, no. 41 (Winter 1981/82), pp. 134–53.

19. *Washington Post*, 19 June 1981. The United States also temporarily suspended the delivery of four F-16 fighter bombers to Israel.

20. *ABC News*, 'Issues and Answers', 28 June 1981; and *Time* (19 July 1982).

21. This cleared the way for the US Department of State to approve export licences for the sale of six civilian versions of C130 Hercules transport planes to Iraq despite strong congressional opposition. *The Times*, 28 May 1982.

22. The Soviet Union sold the Shah military equipment costing more than $1 billion. The arms bought from Moscow, and now supplied by Eastern Europe and other Soviet allies, include Katyusha rocket artillery, surface-to-air missiles, anti-aircraft guns, armoured personnel carriers, small arms and anti-tank missiles. By 1978 the Shah's government was operating a factory to produce the RPG-7 anti-tank missile, and this factory was functioning by March 1982. *New York Times*, 8 March 1982.

23. It is estimated that the air force storage areas alone contained 20 to 30 million aircraft or helicopter spare parts. These large amounts of spare parts and ammunitions were theoretically 'lost' when the pre-revolutionary computer storage in Iran ceased to function. Evidently the Iranians succeeded in mapping out the storage areas and put the spare parts to use. *Washington Post*, 8 April 1982.

24. US Department of State, Press Release, no. 177, 26 May 1982.

25. *Washington Post*, 27 May 1982.

26. *New York Times*, 26 Sept. 1980.

27. In a Kremlin speech in honour of President Reddy of India. Ibid., 1 Oct. 1980.

28. *Washington Post*, 28 Sept. 1980.

29. First proposed in a speech to the Indian parliament. *New York Times*, 11 Dec. 1980. The same proposal was repeated in a speech to the 26th CPSU Congress. *New York Times*, 24 Feb. 1981.

30. *Washington Post*, 11 Oct. 1980.

31. *New York Times*, 3 Feb. 1980 and 28 Sept. 1980.

32. *Washington Post*, 3 March 1981.

33. *Report of the Central Committee of the CPSU to the XXVI Congress of the Communist Party of the Soviet Union and the Immediate Tasks of the Party in Home and Foreign Policy, 23 Feb. 1981* (Novosti Press Agency Publishing House, Moscow, 1981), p. 23.

34. *The Times*, 6 Oct. 1980.

35. *Washington Post*, 16 Feb. 1981.

36. For examples of this theme, see *Foreign Broadcast Information Service/ USSR International Affairs* (FBIS/USST), 1 July 1981, p. H3, and *FBIS/USSR*, 11 Sept. 1981, pp. H1–H2.

37. Alvin Z. Rubinstein, 'The Soviet Union and Iran under Khomeini', *International Affairs* (Autumn 1981), pp. 612–13.

38. *FBIS/USSR*, 10 March 1982, pp. H1–H2.

39. *New York Times*, 21 Dec. 1981. *The Times*, 5 May 1983.

40. *Washington Post*, 5 May 1981.

41. Ibid., 19 April 1981.

42. Ibid., 5 May 1981 and 4 Nov. 1980.

43. Ibid., 11 Oct. 1980. See also *Middle East Economic Digest* (16–22 Oct. 1981).

44. Aside from the alleged savagery of this inconclusive war, press reports indicate that loss of life on both sides has been high. One estimate puts the losses of the first 26 months of fighting at 200,000 soldiers dead from both sides while 70,000 more have been taken prisoner. *Time* (11 Oct. 1982).

9 REGIONAL AND WORLDWIDE IMPLICATIONS OF THE GULF WAR

John Duke Anthony

Introduction

Considering the regional and worldwide implications of the Iran-Iraq war is reminiscent of John Dewey's observation that 'a sculptor may see many different figures in a block of stone'. So, too, may an analyst view the present Gulf war from many different perspectives. Defence and security specialists who perceive the importance of a balance of forces in the region, for example, have been unable to determine the exact military nature of the conflict inasmuch as neither combatant to date has demonstrated the ability to inflict a decisive defeat upon the other. Other observers, who minimize the significance of the confrontation between the two countries' armed forces, insist that the larger implications of the struggle stem from the Sunni-Shi'a religious differences between Iran and Iraq — and among Muslims elsewhere in the region. Still others have been acutely apprehensive all along about the possibility of increased superpower involvement in the conflict.

All of this is but to say that the regional and worldwide implications of the conflict to date have been and remain characterized by extreme complexity. Such phenomena are all the more confusing in the midst of the disorder accompanying any war in progress. Hence, any analyst of its implications must contend with a myriad of sometimes not-so-obviously related forces and factors. While these phenomena may at times appear quite vague and inseparable, a tentative assessment of the war may be reached if one but gauges the respective responses to the war by outside parties.

Evolution of the War

Perceptions of the war to date have passed through at least six stages. In the first, there was a widespread perception among the Arab Gulf states that the war might sooner or later involve everyone in the region. This was the inspiration behind the early *de facto* move of these states to align themselves with Iraq. Kuwait, Saudi Arabia, the Emirates and Oman, for example, indicated their willingness to extend important logistical and financial support to Iraq only days after the fighting erupted.

Perceptions later entered a second stage, whereby these same states reasoned that it was indeed possible to remain detached from the actual military dimensions of the conflict and let the two protagonists fight it out between themselves. A major reason was Western diplomatic intervention during the early stages of the war, which resulted in Iraq's curtailing its earlier intentions to wrest control from Iran of three disputed islands near the mouth of the Gulf. For the next fourteen months, maritime traffic through the strategic Strait of Hormuz remained relatively unimpeded; US-dispatched AWACS airplanes to Saudi Arabia served to bolster the air surveillance and defence capabilities of a considerable portion of the Gulf's southern littoral, and foreign access to, and local production and export of, the non-combatants' petroleum resources continued apace.

A third phase came with the December 1981 *coup* attempt in Bahrain, which illuminated much more clearly than previously the broad implications of the war. The conflict was still perceived as confined to Iraq and Iran, but it began to carry with it a potential for some kind of Sunni-Shi'a confrontation on a scale much broader than envisaged earlier. A fourth phase evolved when a number of radical Arab states — Syria, Libya and South Yemen — plus Israel and North Korea, extended various forms of political and military support to Iran. This demonstrated to some analysts that the afore-mentioned third phase, which had seemed to raise the spectre of sectarian conflict, had also effected a coalition of radical Arab states and such unlikely bedfellows as Israel and North Korea in opposition to the moderate-to-conservative alliance backing the heretofore-considered radical Iraq. To still other analysts, these developments were less relevant or significant than the irony of such countries as Soviet-supported Syria, Libya, and South Yemen, together with Israel, aligning themselves with Iran not so much in pursuit of radicalism, but rather as a manifestation of anti-Iraqi sentiments. This has placed the regional role and involvement of the USSR in a position quite unlike any in recent memory.

A fifth phase began in July 1982 with the Iranian invasion of

Iraq. Tehran's motivation in this endeavour probably was to obtain a better bargaining position in the eventual settlement. But Iraq succeeded in repulsing the Iranian forces. Finally, a sixth phase evolved after the failure of the Iranian invasion, and the war reached a military and diplomatic stalemate with no end in sight to this inconclusive situation.

Some Strategic Considerations

Among the many regional and global implications associated with the conflict to date, the war has served to highlight for some analysts the view that Iraq, in geostrategic terms, is in some ways less significant strategically to the Gulf states, the Soviet Union and the West than is Iran. Such analysts consider that as far as the Gulf is concerned, Iraqi ambitions to play a regional security role are seriously constrained by its having the shortest littoral of any of the eight Gulf states: less than fifty miles, with most of that lying in shallow water and of uncertain access and sovereignty — the latter resulting from Iraq's territorial disputes with both Kuwait and Iran.

Iran is seen by contrast as sharing not only contested land and water frontiers with Iraq, but also offshore boundaries with the entire north Arabian peninsula littoral across its more than six-hundred-mile coast from the Shatt al-Arab all the way to Pakistan. Iraq, moreover, lacks Iran's strategic significance due to the latter's position astride the nothern shores of the Strait of Hormuz, through which passes the bulk of the oil bound for sale on the international market. Thus, on the matter of applying laws of the sea to international waterways, it is Iran's policies, not those of Iraq, that matter most in regional as well as international councils. If Iraq were to prove unable to secure its own border with Iran, let alone make good its claim for undisputed sovereignty over the strategic Shatt al-Arab waterway — the country's only outlet to the sea — how much less credible, in the eyes of many analysts, would be its pretensions to a leadership role in matters of regional security.

In addition, for Bahrain, Sharjah and Ras al-Khaima, the issue of Iranian irredentism is a serious one. The matter of maritime boundaries between Iran and the Gulf Co-operation Council (GCC) states in general is either in legal limbo or regarded as unsatisfactory by one or more of the parties concerned. In other instances, demographic considerations and their linkage to internal security rank uppermost among the anxieties which the Gulf war has occasioned throughout the region. Despite the fear of an Iranian attempt to export revolution to the south side of the Gulf, however, Iran's actions for the first two years following the ousting of the Shah have been mainly rhetorical.

To be sure, during that period there were incidents of Khomeini's lieutenants inciting Shi'a militants in Bahrain, Kuwait and the Emirates. In each instance, the militants demanded changes in the local political and social systems in order to elevate their status to one more nearly equal to that of the Sunni segment of the populace. None of the disturbances occasioned by such opposition groups during that time, however, came close to provoking the kind of reaction that occurred in December 1981. On that occasion, Iranian complicity was uncovered in a *coup* attempt in Bahrain, led mainly by some 70 Bahraini nationalists plus a dozen Saudi citizens of Shi'a persuasion from the Kingdom's Eastern Province, along with one or two Kuwaitis and Omanis.

Iraq's global geostrategic significance likewise pales in comparison with Iran's. The Soviet Union, for example, borders not Iraq but Iran; and it is no small neighbour, with more than 1,500 miles of common frontier. The day-to-day interaction between Iranian and Soviet citizens probably exceeds that of the Soviet Union with any other Middle Eastern people.

Iraq may have a longer and more comprehensive military relationship with Moscow than does Iran; Libya, Ethiopia and Syria may more effectively serve Soviet ideological and related interests in North and East Africa as well as in the eastern Mediterranean; and South Yemen, in addition to ideological compatibility, may better serve important Soviet needs for access to and a physical presence in the Horn of Africa–Red Sea regions. But none of these countries, in the final analysis, has the global or regional geostrategic significance that characterizes Iran. For these and other reasons pertaining to strategic concerns, the nature and orientation of any Iranian regime, and thus its regional and global role, have never been treated lightly by the superpowers.

Military Uncertainties

It has not been conclusively determined thus far which of the combatants is militarily stronger. Although Iran is clearly the greater in size and overall population, it remains to be seen whether this can or will be translated into an unmitigated defeat of Iraq. Early in 1982 Syria closed its frontier with Iraq. That leaves open only the routes to and from Iraq by way of Jordan, Turkey, Kuwait or Saudi Arabia. In theory, then, Iran could rely on economic strangulation rather than a deep military incursion to achieve its aims in Iraq.

If clear military victory of either party alone seems improbable, an external factor may be Turkish and Egyptian interests. Turkey, the most militarily powerful Islamic Middle Eastern state, a member of NATO and a neighbour of both countries, is opposed to an Iranian invasion and occupation of Iraq and may intervene if its own national security and related interests are endangered. Egypt, still regarded by many as the most militarily powerful Arab country, is also opposed to Iran in this context and has already enhanced Iraq's prospects for resisting Iran.

Foreign Assistance

Throughout the war, Iran has had more limited outside assistance than Iraq. To date, Tehran's main supporters have been Syria, Libya, South Yemen, North Korea and Israel. Some Kremlin officials undoubtedly regard Iran as the greater strategic plum and retain the hope that some way might be found to further Soviet interests there. Yet Moscow has not had a free hand so far in choosing whether or not to support Iran directly. A potentially enormous cost of heavy Soviet assistance is that it could easily be viewed by most of the more than 20 Arab states as hostile towards their own interests.

In addition, the Soviet Union has its own domestic restraints. It has a vested interest, for example, in not becoming over-extended or precipitously involved in events beyond its borders, given the leadership succession question at home, plus uncertainties along its European and Asian frontiers. Moscow's recent behaviour indicates that it will not allow events among client states to exceed the point where it might be obligated to intervene on their behalf.

A further constraint to Soviet intervention thus far has been the nature and orientation of the Iranian regime. Many question the extent of a Soviet inclination to intervene in support of a regime in Tehran which is neither communist nor socialist, nor likely, in its current make-up, to extend a significant degree of recognition or tolerance to either ideology. Beyond the insecure political climate in Iran, staying the hand of the would-be interventionist further is lack of a sufficiently mass-based, pro-Soviet political constituency — however tolerated — and notwithstanding the existence of the communist Tudeh party.

Just as Iran's many geostrategic attributes warrant ongoing Soviet attention in connection with Moscow's hopes to enhance Soviet global and regional interests, so is the reverse argument also valid. To wit: Iran, far more than Iraq, is capable of destabilizing an important region inside the Soviet Union — the Central Asian Soviets — because its Islamic perspective is closer than Iraq's Baathist outlook to the sentiments of the Soviet Union's Muslim citizens. In the absence of the above-mentioned grass-roots support, it cannot be ruled out that a Soviet intervention against the Khomeini regime in Iran could result in as much domestic harm inside the Soviet Union as in strategic benefits of a tangible nature.

The prospects for Soviet intervention in Iraq have been similarly bleak. Moscow is without a secure political base there as well, not only with regard to the Baath party's entrenched position in the government, but also, as in Iran, without a mass-based, well-organized constituency which is favourably inclined towards the Soviet Union.

Meanwhile, it is unlikely that the Gulf states will be able to finance Iraq in the period ahead as they have been for the first two years of the war. Israel's invasion of Lebanon in June 1982 resulted in demands from Syria, Lebanon and the Palestinians for massive amounts of economic assistance at a time when, due to dwindling financial surpluses and depressed market conditions in the petroleum industry, the Gulf states were without the kinds of resources that were previously at their disposal. In addition, were Syria to succeed in its request for large-scale financing from Saudi Arabia in return for accommodating in Syria a portion of the Palestinian leadership, this could affect the regional balance between Syria and Iraq. Nonetheless, Saudi Arabia, Kuwait, the UAE and Qatar, all of which have reason to fear Khomeini-inspired *coup* attempts by their own Shi'a Muslims, have already pumped more than $25 billion into Iraq's war effort, and perhaps would contribute equally massive sums to reach a settlement that, in the best of worlds, would accomplish two objectives: an end to the daily possibility of an Iranian air strike on one of their oil installations and an end to Tehran-inspired attempts to spread the fundamentalist Shi'a movement to the south side of the Gulf.

There is reason, however, to believe that Iraq will be in need of various kinds of assistance from the West if it is to defend itself credibly against Iran. To do this, it would not be surprising if Baghdad cancelled the 1972 Soviet-Iraqi treaty of friendship. The treaty, to be sure, has remained dormant since both parties disregarded one of its most important clauses — the obligation of one signatory to inform and consult with the other in advance of any military action — when the Soviet Union invaded Afghanistan and Iraq invaded Iran, respectively.

It is unlikely that Iraq would be able to receive direct assistance from the United States, due to the widespread public image in the US of the Baghdad regime as one which continues to harbour and sponsor terrorists. Compounding the difficulty is that, in contrast to the regime in Tehran, Iraq has had a far longer and more multi-faceted relationship with the Soviet Union, with which the Reagan administration is considerably more preoccupied — many would say obsessed — than any US presidency in a quarter of a century. However much Iraq might wish it were otherwise, and hope that the American public as well as US policy might recognize and reward the change in Iraq's international posture in recent years, the legacy of earlier days when most Americans perceived Iraqis as 'bad guys' lives on in Washington.

There is ample regional precedent for the renunciation by an Arab state of a close identification with one or the other super-power. Syria's rupture with the United States, for example, was viewed both regionally and further afield as necessary and expedient in view of Damascus's shift in orientation towards the Soviet Union. A more dramatic, recent and memorable example, however, was Egypt's severance in 1972 of the close relationship between Cairo and Moscow, as a prelude to turning towards the United States. What these previous examples of abrupt regional-global realignment suggest is that if Iraq does in fact find itself in need of assistance from the West in the near future, it may prove more convenient and expedient for Baghdad to turn to a European state, such as France, with Saudi Arabia and the other Gulf states paying the bill.

Ideology

Many of the implications for possible foreign involvement in this war may turn on the progress of the ideological warfare between the combatants. In this context, many have argued that Iraq is at a distinct ideological disadvantage; they see its Baathist ideology as secular, Western and imported, without any enduring impact to date on the majority of the country's population. By contrast, Iranian ideology is both more indigenous in its roots and more pervasive in its extent, rendering it a far greater challenge to several governments in the region. Given the relatively low literacy rates in both countries, it is only natural that a homegrown variety of Islamic ideology would have greater appeal. In the simplest terms, large masses of people in both countries can and do identify with it, including many of the educated elites.

It is apparent that Khomeini makes little distinction between Saddam Hussein and the Baath party as a whole. Although some Iranian demands have called for his overthrow, others have indicated that the entire party would have to step down before Iran would agree to a cessation of armed hostilities. The reason for the ambiguous distinction made between Saddam Hussein as head of state on one hand, and the Baath party as the basis of the government on the other, may be, as many have claimed, that Khomeini has all along believed fervently that Iraq is destined to become the next Islamic Republic. By all accounts, it has so far been a source of major dismay and disappointment to him that Iraq, with its majority Shi'a population and the strong cultural ties with Iran of many of its inhabitants, has not yet produced such an Islamic Republic. And Tehran has doubtlessly counted on an anticipated measure of disaffection among Iraq's Shi'a Muslims against Sunni Saddam Hussein in their thrust to unseat him.

Regional Security Implications

Among the more immediate concerns of the Arab Gulf states since the outbreak of the war has been the awareness that both their national security and the jugular of their economic well-being could be dealt a devastating blow literally within minutes by actions taken by one or other of the two combatants. The need to find a more credible and effective means to deal with the pressing problem of security was, indeed, one of the most compelling reasons for establishing the Gulf Co-operation Council (GCC) in 1981. Cultural, sectarian, ideological and demographic issues are also at stake.

The reaction of Saudi Arabia to the Iran-Iraq war has been quite different from that of the other Gulf states. The Riyadh regime has been and remains profoundly disturbed by the Sunni-Shi'a character of the war. Not only has Saudi Arabia usually aligned itself with the traditionalist side of the Sunni Muslim camp, but the fundamentalist foundation of its own regime is the repository of a very different ideology, although in the eyes of many, it is a no less radical interpretation of Islam. Thus, on the sectarian level, Saudi Arabia is especially concerned about the potential of the Tehran government to undermine the Kingdom's regional role. Qatar's reaction has been similar to that of Riyadh.

Kuwait has also had numerous reasons to worry about the war, but for different reasons than Saudi Arabia. Being a closer neighbour to both combatants than Saudi Arabia, having already been bombed several times by Iranian pilots, and lying far more exposed than any other non-combatant due to its crucial logistical role in channelling supplies to Iraq from abroad, Kuwait has been living as dangerously as any GCC state these past 30 months. Kuwait's position in the Baghdad versus Tehran ideological competition has also been different. It is developing as a secular rather than a sectarian state, overtly sympathetic neither to the Saudi Arabian brand of Islam nor to the Iranian interpretation; nor has it been anti-Sunni or anti-Shi'a in its policies and actions.

In terms of the UAE, one has seen, in effect, a replay of Kuwaiti policy, in other words, successfully managing relations with a far more powerful neighbour despite the difficulties emerging out of an asymmetrical power situation. Just as Kuwait has managed to co-exist with Iraq, so has the UAE managed to co-exist with Iran despite disputed claims over islands. In addition, the UAE and Kuwait have built up a reservoir of international goodwill in return for the vast number of economic favours they have provided others through the generosity of their foreign economic assistance programmes — assistance which they have astutely intertwined with ongoing support for their own independence and territorial integrity.

Bahrain, on the other hand, is a special case. As the Arab world's only island state and one of the few Gulf states which lacks the financial wherewithal to ingratiate itself with others through aid programmes, Bahrain remains acutely apprehensive about the implications of the war for its unique population; as in Iraq, a clear majority of Bahrain's Muslim inhabitants are Shi'a, but the government itself, much as in the incumbent regime in Iraq, is dominated by Sunnis. Oman, which occupies a position on the Strait of Hormuz that puts it in a different situation from that of the other GCC members, has been the Gulf state least worried about the Sunni-Shi'a dimension of the war. The Shi'a population of Oman is not indigenous, but consists rather of longstanding emigrant communities from Southern Iraq, Bahrain, Pakistan and India. In further contrast to most of the other Gulf states, the implications of the war for Omani national security and related interests have centred mainly on matters of a strategic nature. Muscat has voiced little concern, for example, about the Islamic nature and orientation of the Tehran government. Rather, its abiding concern has been whether the course of the war might give Tehran cause to rely to a greater extent on the Soviet Union.

In addition to the Arab states of the Gulf, Pakistan — as an Islamic country bordering Iran — figures in the regional security equation. It is important to stress that the Pakistani government has indicated on innumerable occasions that it will not involve its military forces in any combat against Muslim people. The government in Islamabad is still smarting from the process of helping King Hussein in September 1970, when the Jordanian army was fighting Palestinian guerrillas. Although Pakistani units did not take part in the fighting, there is little doubt that individual Pakistani soldiers, whether as trainers or instructors, got caught up in the fighting with particular units and found themselves in the midst of a conflict with fellow Muslims, in this instance, Palestinians. It is unlikely that Pakistan would commit its armed forces to a conflict with Iran, due to the neighbourly relations and underlying affinity between the two peoples: they are much closer to one another than either is to neighbouring Arab nations.

At a lesser level of threat, however, it is possible that the Pakistanis might be willing to use force inside Saudi Arabia if a source of trouble were to arise in one of the regions of the Kingdom, or if it became necessary to guard the oilfields or the holy sites in Mecca. At present Saudi Arabia is said to be financing one or more Pakistani special forces divisions in Pakistan, but with an extra mandate for regional intervention in one of the GCC states should the need arise.

Iraq, due to its Sunni minority regime as compared with Iran's Shi'a majority rule, poses far less of an ideological challenge to regional security than does Iran. This marks a significant shift from the not very distant past, when the predominantly Sunni Arab Gulf states had reason to be more concerned by Iraq's numerous *coups* and revolutionary rhetoric than were assured by the Sunni composition of its regime. In addition, the constraints on intervention elsewhere in the Gulf by either of the two combatants are considerably stronger in Iraq than in Iran, for President Saddam Hussein is confronted by ongoing domestic opposition on one hand, and is vulnerable to the unpredictable actions of Khomeini and the financial largesse of the Arab Gulf states on the other. All of this shortens Iraq's political leash. The Arab Gulf states, for their part, are well aware that should the current Iraqi government fall, it could be replaced by one much more threatening to their security than the incumbent regime. Despite the foregoing, Gulf Arab security concerns have been alleviated in the eyes of some since Iraq, under Saddam Hussein, has leaned increasingly toward the West, even while Iran, under the Khomeini regime, has been doing its utmost to wrench away.

For the West as well as the other Gulf states, the consequence is that the more worrisome of the two countries is clearly Iran, not Iraq. For example, as Iran has moved away from the other Gulf states, Iraq has moved towards them. This has been reflected in Iraq's steadily improved relations with Saudi Arabia, reduced tensions with Kuwait, and a virtual end to Iraqi support of the Popular Front for the Liberation of Oman. Indeed, since Khomeini came to power, Iraq has forged a broad range of co-operative ties with other Gulf states aimed at enhancing their respective capabilities against Iranian-sponsored infiltration activities. In many other ways as well, Iraq, though not a GCC member, has adopted policies and taken actions on issues of regional importance that have been complementary to GCC needs.

The Iranian revolution and civil war, as well as Iraq's failure to win a quick or decisive victory against Iran, has kept Iraq committed to improved relations with the other Arab Gulf states and Jordan, upon which Iraq will have to rely increasingly for economic and logistical support — to the tune of more than $22 billion thus far — whether the war continues or reaches a settlement.

Not all Iraqis have discarded the view, articulated with some force by a group of Baathists to this writer a year before the war began, that Iraqi victory over Khomeini-led Iran could enhance rather than endanger Western interests in the Arab world, most notably among the six GCC states, and in Jordan and Egypt as well. However debatable such a proportion may be, those who maintain this view emphasize that the setback for Western and Gulf states' interests which would occur, should Iran defeat Iraq, is beyond question.

Those upon whom Iraq remains most dependent for supplies, loans and mediation efforts to bring the war to a rapid end — in other words, the Gulf's non-combatant Arab states — have an interest in seeing that Iraq does not emerge from the conflict with the capacity or intent to export its own radical ideology to land beyond its shores.

By contrast, those outside the region who have helped Iran in the conflict would not necessarily view with disfavour an Iran which might, when the war is over, serve as a greater inspiration than it already has for radical and revolutionary forces operating in and adjacent to the Arab Gulf states. Iraq has neither the stated intent nor the individual conduits at hand for such actions. But Iran, in addition to its considerable advantage over Iraq in terms of geography and military forces available for these purposes, has both.

This was sufficiently demonstrated by the 1981 *coup* attempt in Bahrain. Not knowing whether other groups might also be training inside Iran for future strikes at a Gulf regime, and, if so, how many and/or which GCC state might be the next target, the Gulf states, with Saudi Arabia at the forefront, reacted swiftly. Within a week, Riyadh and Bahrain had signed a collective security pact designed for consultation and mutual military assistance in the event of any similar incident occurring in the future. Qatar signed a nearly identical agreement with Saudi Arabia shortly therafter, and within two months the remaining GCC states had entered into similar arrangements.

If Iran should press on in its invasion of Iraq, the other Gulf states will have no choice but to reassess seriously their previous thinking about regional security. Iraq, meanwhile, will probably have to find its own means of security. It may find it convenient for the time being to continue working through Egyptian-US and other channels, with a view to reaching an understanding with Western countries on the strategic situation in the Gulf.

At the more immediate level of armaments, Iraq has little choice but to turn to Europe, relying on the supportive financial assistance coming primarily from the GCC states; otherwise, Iraq cannot count on military support from any of the other Arab Gulf states. In its current battle with Iran, Iraq therefore stands alone in the Gulf. Even a differently constituted Syrian government in Damascus can be ruled out as a potential arms supplier at any time in the foreseeable future, not only for previous longstanding political and ideological reasons, but for the more immediate considerations evolving from its six-year preoccupation in Lebanon. In the final analysis, there are only two regional states, Egypt and Turkey, from which Iraq can entertain even minimal hopes of some form of military assistance, albeit not much more than resupplies.

With the foregoing backdrop to the regional situation, two contradictory theories have emerged as to the response of the other Gulf states in the event of an Iranian victory. According to the first, if Tehran becomes more and more dominant in its campaign to continue carrying the war into Iraq with the intent of overthrowing the Baathist regime there, the other Gulf states may begin distancing themselves from the United States so as to curry favour with Tehran and thereby diminish the sense of threat from that capital.

The second theory is that the GCC states may conclude that Iran's objectives preclude a relaxation in tension at any point in the foreseeable future, regardless of what kinds of foreign policy initiatives they may undertake. In this context, the view is that 'whatever we might do would not be enough in the eyes of Tehran, so we had better try to become more secure. Only in this way do we have any hope of the threat being lessened.' For those who feel and argue this way, there is only one credible choice at their disposal: closer military ties with Western countries.

Many may conclude that the latter line of thinking is a nonoption due to the political disrepute in which the United States is held by the overwhelming majority of the people in the region. The proponents of this school of thought, however, argue that priorities are priorities, and the need to survive is of such basic significance as to override what, by contrast, they hold to be more ephemeral considerations. Western countries are the only ones with the means, and at the same time the mutuality of interest, as well as a pre-existing network of compatible equipment on the ground in the GCC states, to afford a credible policy option for enhanced strategic co-operation with these states.

All of this and more, to be sure, hinges directly and immediately on the outcome of events simultaneously taking place in Lebanon. In this regard, the visible association of the United States with the Palestinians in a positive context — for example, by announcing unequivocal support for Palestinian self-determination and/or entering into an open dialogue with the PLO leadership — would provide an essential element for improving any military relationship between the US and the states of the region. If Washington emerges from the current negotiations concerning Lebanon worse off than before, however, it is quite probable that either the Shi'a elements in a number of the GCC states or the resident Palestinian communities — and in some instances, possibly both — will turn on their host governments, managing in the process to elicit a fair amount of support from the indigenous Arab citizenry.

Minorities

The activities of the numerous groups in Iran which had previously endeavoured to win a measure of autonomy, if not secession, from the central government in Tehran have all been held in abeyance, as it were, since the war erupted. One reason has been that the overwhelming majority of Iranians, without regard to ethnic identity, class or sectarian orientation, appear to have coalesced in what is, in essence, a national effort to defend the homeland in the face of the original Iraqi invasion.

An equally telling factor, however, has been that wars tend to create rather cruel conditions; that is, governments tend to bury any source of domestic trouble which, in their eyes, might pose a threat to the successful pursuit of the struggle. In time of peace, governments often respond to rebellious activity on the part of their citizenry with a minimum of force. In time of war, by contrast, the tendency has been for governments to use maximum brutality to defeat such rebels and brand them as traitors. Given this reality and the almost certain response of either of the two governments in this matter, rebellious factions in both countries have been exceptionally cautious in their behaviour since the war broke out.

It is, of course, important to stress the fact that Iraq is not immune from such phenomena; with particular respect to its

Kurdish population, it has had greater experience than Iran in dealing with this kind of problem. Nonetheless, should Iran lose the war, Saddam Hussein may anticipate renewed heavy support by Iran for the Kurds in Iraq.

Iran's minority problems, by contrast, are more complex than Iraq's because:

(1) The groups are larger in number, both in category and in overall size (Kurds, Turkish-speaking Iranians, Arabs and Baluchis, to name the most prominent).
(2) They reside in areas some distance — and in different directions — from the capital.
(3) The uncertainty of the central government in Tehran as to whether it will be able to come to terms with these groups, and *vice versa*, is both greater and more recent. The question has been held in abeyance for the past 30 months primarily because of the war with Iraq.

Despite the foregoing, one of the implications for Iran's minorities may be the option of resuming active pursuit of their aspirations once the war is ended. If so, might one or more of the minorities in question consider turning to outside groups for assistance: to the Soviet Union, for example, or to kindred groups in Pakistan, Afghanistan and the GCC states? If so, what might be the response? Would the Soviets be able and/or inclined to extend to any of these groups the kind of aid that they provided, from their presence in South Yemen, for the insurgents in Oman's southern province of Dhofar? And were they to do so, what might be the expected result? Would this be likely to set off a conflict different from any which has involved the Soviet Union and/or other non-Gulf powers in the region to date?

Conversely, were the insurgents to receive aid from non-Soviet sources, what kinds of problems might this entail? More specifically, if insurgents thus aided were to begin to pose a serious threat to the Iranian regime, might that regime, or its successor, in order to survive, be inclined to accept foreign assistance in quelling the insurrection? In such a scenario, might a country such as the Soviet Union, citing insecurity on its southern flank, be inclined to intervene without regard to the niceties associated with whether or not a formal invitation had been extended?

When the war comes to an end, there will therefore be reason to query the fate of such groups. Will they renew pressure for greater autonomy and/or a greater voice in the national government? If so, would it be the policy of central government to be accommodating or confrontational? If at all the latter, to what extent might this compel one or more of the groups in question to seek external support?

Of the various options and scenarios at hand, if Baluchistan achieved autonomy or pursued secession from Pakistan, this might increase in significance due to the large number of Baluchis in Soviet-dominated Afghanistan. The Baluchis can provide the Soviet Union with a corridor to the sea, and the fact that they are widely dispersed, not only in Pakistan and Iran but throughout the Arab states of the Gulf, makes them potential insurgents. In addition, the Baluchis are renowned fighters and are regarded as among the most economically resourceful of any minority in the region. Even so, the Soviet Union might well recognize the sagacity of holding in readiness any Baluchi cards which it may possess, with the prospect of using them in the absence of an agreeable relationship at government level.

Linkage

The current situation defies the certainty of precise analysis due to the constantly changing events in the eastern Mediterranean, most particularly in Lebanon, but also in the West Bank and Gaza. Looking down the road, if peace is established in Lebanon and the Palestinians are engaged in a direct dialogue with the United States, the degree of antagonistic and alienated feelings amongst regimes and people alike towards the United States would diminish. This could have a comprehensive and altogether salutary impact on the region, substantially weakening the export appeal of Iran's fundamentalist revolution in the process, especially if the Palestinians are seen to be part of process in which the United States is playing a positive role.

On the other hand, if the reverse were to occur, a backlash could be anticipated against the existing moderate regimes, and this could only work to the benefit of Tehran. When Iran crossed into Iraq it was a net gain for Israel in that it diverted the attention of the Arab Gulf states away from Lebanon. And Iran advanced its own cause and embarrassed the Arab regimes by being the first — and only —

regional state to provide actual military assistance to the Syrians, Lebanese and Palestinians in the Israeli onslought in the summer of 1982. This is all the more ironic with regard to the Iran-Israel relationship. Although hard evidence of collusion between Iran and Israel has been elusive to date, each has seen an advantage in operating under cover of the other's military moves, and Israel has been central to Tehran's ability to prolong the war by sending weapons and spare parts.

For their part, the Arab states of the Gulf are acutely conscious of the broad range of regional security problems that these events have occasioned, and they are cognizant of the need to broaden the base of strategic co-operation with Western countries. With regard to the military most powerful of these Western countries, however, they continue to be constrained by heavy US support for Israel, even as Israel persists in expropriating and annexing increasing amounts of Arab land while simultaneously denying Palestinian self-determination.

No Arab state, much less any Gulf state with an influential Palestinian presence, can much longer afford to ignore or avoid challenging the extent to which the US backs Israel and the concomitant erosion of American credibility and regional capabilities. This is especially true today, as those Arab states which have reluctantly taken over Lebanon's role of host to the Palestinian leadership may find themselves confronted with increasingly restless Palestinian civilians already living within their borders.

Diplomacy

There have been numerous unsuccessful attempts by third parties — the United Nations, the Islamic Conference Organization, non-aligned groups, and Turkey, Pakistan and Algeria — to find a peaceful settlement to the war. Apart from emphasizing that the US 'has remained from the beginning, and will remain, neutral in the war', official US policy has been 'supportive of the independence and territorial integrity of both Iran and Iraq', and opposed to the seizure of territory by force, and has reiterated the need for 'an immediate end to hostilities, and a negotiated settlement'.

A formal White House statement of 14 July 1982 declared US support for the security of friendly states in the region which might feel threatened by the conflict, and announced that the United States was prepared to consult with those states in the region which might feel threatened by the conflict on appropriate steps to ensure their security. Statements of intent aside, the US has no formal diplomatic relations with either Iraq or Iran, although some American diplomats are in Iraq. This makes the war especially frustrating for Washington, because although the outcome could be potentially so serious for Western and moderate Arab interests in the Gulf, the US claims to hold little sway over the course of hostilities, despite its means and obligation to constrain Israeli support for a crucial aspect of the Iranian war effort.

Europe, meanwhile, has been distancing itself from the political quagmire of the Middle East and devoting itself more and more to European problems. To the extent that the Europeans remain involved in the Middle East, it is overwhelmingly in the context of economic interest. European statesmen apply the proper and locally much-appreciated rhetoric on political questions; but such action has done little to influence US policies and actions on the question of Palestine. Similarly, with regard to bringing the Iran-Iraq war to a close, the Europeans have had little impact to date. An exception, of course, was the mediation effort by the Swedish Prime Minister Olof Palme between November 1980 and February 1981. The Palme mission, however, was premature and of only marginal significance.

The history of Iraqi-Iranian relations — as well as those of other Middle Eastern countries — demonstrates that only when the two countries themselves are ready for an agreement can other parties play a role. On no occasion in this or earlier conflicts has a unilateral mediation effort by outside parties brought results of any lasting benefit. An example is the Algiers Agreement of March 1975, when the Shah and Saddam Hussein met in Algiers and signed an accord to end their long-standing disputes over the Shatt al-Arab, the Kurdish question and Iraqi support for radical movements in the Gulf. Only then, when both states were ready to conclude an agreement, was mediation effective, even if Iraq's Hussein was beleaguered at the time and the Shah was at the height of his power, thereby lending credence to the view of many that the agreement was adhered to by Baghdad under circumstances akin to duress.

Until recently, as is now well known, neither country has indicated a readiness to resolve the current dispute. As a result, international initiatives to end the war have provided one or some-times both of the countries with opportunities to exploit such initiatives for their own purposes. On the Iraqi side, the war in Lebanon in summer 1982 provided Baghdad with its first con-venient opportunity for more concerted efforts to conclude the war diplomatically. By doing so, it hoped to avoid the far higher domestic costs which could be expected to be borne by either country in the event of a military defeat. Perhaps Iraq was hopeful that a diplomatic settlement could be achieved before the the the Non-Aligned Conference, which was scheduled to open in Baghdad on 6 September 1982. But the fighting continued and the conference was transferred to New Delhi.

On the Iranian side, Tehran's confidence has shown itself defiantly in recent weeks — first by refusing to comply with Arab-led call in OPEC for ceilings on individual oil production by the main producers, and second by rejecting Iraq's offer of a limited ceasefire in the Nowruz area to allow technicians to repair the damaged Iranian oil-wells at the head of the Gulf. The Iranians have flatly rejected any UN actions to end the dispute, giving as their reason the fact that the UN made no effort to intervene when Iraq had the upper hand.

Policy Considerations

If the foregoing attests only in part to the numerous regional and worldwide inplications of the conflict to date, it nonetheless indicates several directions that policy formulation might be expected to take in the near future. In terms of Western concerns, a major theme had clearly come to be the degree to which the intensi-fication of the war, on the one hand, and mounting evidence of aggressive Iranian intentions against virtually every Arab Gulf government, on the other, posed direct and immediate challenges to Western strategic, economic and political interests.

Secondly, while a neutral Western response to Iraq's 1980 invasion of an Iran which was still holding the US hostages was seen as only appropriate in the eyes of most Western analysts, the continuation of such a policy in light of the reversal of the war and Iran's increasing anti-Western vehemence was viewed by many of the same observers as counter-productive to the interests of Western countries, the Arab Gulf states and most other Arab countries.

Thirdly, all Western countries with interests at stake in the outcome of the conflict have indicated that they see little choice but to ensure that Iraq has the capability to withstand a sustained Iranian invasion. Such steps as these powers have considered undertaking towards this goal have included: (1) providing assurance that Iraq would receive adequate military equipment and supplies, including additional shipments through Arab states friendly to Iraq (an example was a British-facilitated $400 million arms transaction through Egypt in the spring of 1982); (2) recommending that the United States normalize diplomatic relations with Iraq and support an intensification of diplomatic efforts to end the conflict; and (3) urging the US to call Israel unequivocally to account for violating US laws in the process of helping Iran — even while Iran held Americans as hostages — with military equipment and spare parts for its predominantly US-manufactured weaponry, most particularly the crucial aid which Tel Aviv supplied the Iranian air force.

A number of subsidiary themes have commanded attention as well. Prominent among these has been acknowledgement by many that so long as the Khomeini regime remains virulently anti-West, there may be little the West can do in the short run aside from not radically altering its relationship with Iraq to such an extent that a later improvement in Western-Iranian ties would be precluded.

In the interim, the most constrained of the Western powers — the US — has limited itself to lending assistance where possible in the construction of a GCC-centred air shield over the Gulf's southern oil fields as a means of guarding against an Iranian threat, and strengthening American 'over-the-horizon' capabilities against the worse case possibility, however remote, that a future Iranian government might seek US help against Soviet intervention.

Influencing the political interests of numerous Western countries was the fact that Iraq, in comparison with Iran, has in recent years become increasingly open to relations with the West in general. Western diplomats were well aware that almost simultaneous with Saddam Hussein's assumption of office, Baghdad initiated a shift in policy away from Moscow. Thousands of Soviet advisors subsequently left Iraq and normal diplomatic relations were being conducted between Baghdad and all of the major Western countries except the US. Further testimony to the reorientation of Iraq's foreign policy in recent years was its severence of diplomatic relations with North Korea and its establishment of consular relations with South Korea in their place.

Western foreign policy officials also seemed to give increasing weight to the fact that, in comparison with Iran, Iraq's economy was clearly the more dynamic of the two. Baghdad had increasingly, in almost ideological aversion to Tehran, intensified its economic ties with the Western world. Politically as well, it was Arab Iraq, not non-Arab Iran, which held a position of leadership among the non-aligned countries, many of which had had long-standing plans to attend the Non-Aligned Conference which was to have been hosted by Iraq.

Finally, and again in terms of any American involvement in settlement of the conflict, it remained a source of widespread concern, one frought with unpredictable regional and global implications, that the US might send troops to protect what it declared at the time of the Carter Doctrine in January 1980 to be its vital interests in the region. At the time of writing, it was in no one's interest — neither that of such global actors as Europe, the US, or the Soviet Union, and, among regional actors, least of all the Gulf states, whether Iraq or Iran or the non-combatants — that such a scenario come to pass. Weighing all costs, regional and global actors alike had every reason to reject further passivity toward this conflict and to ensure that neither the Iranian invasion of Iraq, nor the opposite, would be allowed to succeed.

10 THE PROSPECTS FOR PEACE

Glen Balfour-Paul

This concluding contribution is written with the benefit of some additional months' hindsight. But such changes as have occurred in the scenario are not such as to give this benefit much substance. For the war has dragged on; the declared objectives of the combatants have not conspicuously altered; and the ability of outside agencies to promote a settlement has remained negligible. At first sight then, to speculate on the prospects for peace remains an operation barely more scientific than a Roman talking of auguries. But the attempt must be made.

Before embarking on it, two preliminary definitions are necessary.

First, what in this context do we mean by peace? Are we discussing the prospects merely of hostilities ceasing, of an armistice and a return to barracks? Or do we mean by peace a definitive settlement of the disputed issues? The two are obviously distinct; and though one might lead to the other, it is not even self-evident which must come first. Indeed, the failure of repeated essays in mediation on the part of outside agencies, all based (at least in the first year of the war) on the principle of a ceasefire followed by negotiations for a settlement, might suggest that this natural order of events needs to be reversed: that firing will not cease until the issues are settled. To any such suggestion the retort could be made that rival aspirations which have defied definitive settlement for centuries are unlikely to find one in the immediate future and that firing cannot possibly continue until they do. Be all that as it may, and without prejudging the order of events, it is the prospects of an end to the present war, rather than those of a definitive and lasting settlement, which we shall be examining here.

A second preliminary requirement is a workable definition of what the Iran-Iraq war is all about. For in assessing the prospects of peace, any conclusions we may reach will only be as valid as the premises from which we start. And the premises in this case are the real issues in dispute. So what do we believe them to be? There are broadly three candidates, indicated by the following questions:

(1) Was this war basically just a recrudescence of the age-old rivalry between the states concerned for control over the Shatt al-Arab? And are we to regard their rival claims for the allegiance of Khuzistan/Arabistan as fundamental, or was this just a side-issue thrown in for good measure? Alternatively, and on a wider screen, was this war engaged with the fundamental aim on each side of achieving overall regional hegemony? Or:

(2) Is this war essentially another of the wars of religion, a collision between a currently expansionary and fundamentalist Shi'ism and a secular Sunni-dominated neighbour? Or:

(3) Should we see the clash in much more personal terms? Is this in any significant sense Saddam's War (or, if one prefers, Khomeini's War), something that broke out only because one individual or two individuals so decided?

In short, is this a political war, a secretarian war or a private duel? Clearly, if our answer to this question is wrong, any forecast we may offer of the prospects of peace is likely to be wrong too.

When the Iraqi armed forces first invaded Iran, most outsiders were inclined to identify as the real Iraqi motive (whatever the declared one) a determination to 'topple Khomeini', in the belief that without his personal maleficence things in the region, including Iraq's freedom to pursue its national aims, would return to normal. Khomeini for his part has repeatedly declared, as the war proceeds, that he will not sheath the sword until Saddam Hussein has been put to it, that the removal of Saddam personally from the scene is the fundamental prerequisite for peace. Indeed, on several occasions before the invasion was launched, Khomeini and his lieutenants had called publicly for the liquidation of Saddam.[1] This personalization or personification of the *casus belli* — and each of the two protagonists has reasons enough for personal antipathy — may well contain a measure of truth; and if it were a preponderant measure, all that would be needed for hostilities to end would be the death of Khomeini and/or the replacement of Saddam Hussein: a matter, at most, of time.

But few surely would subscribe to so simplistic a theory. The Trojan War was not, despite Marlowe's great pentameter, caused by the shape of Helen's nose. And while it may be that as long as Saddam Hussein and Khomeini are in power the ending of hostilities is improbable, it does not follow that hostilities would automatically end with their disappearance.

Should we then see it primarily as a religious war? In extreme terms, is Saddam Hussein justified in claiming that Iraq is fighting not just to defend *itself* from Iranian Shi'a subversion or overthrow, but rather to protect the whole community of Sunni Arabs everywhere? Most people, even the Sunni governments of the small Arab states in the immediate vicinity, regarded that claim, advanced in the first flush of war, as an overstatement. Certainly it is in Iraq itself that potential Shi'a disaffection is writ largest; and no one doubts that in the months leading to the outbreak of the war the new Islamic Republic of Iran *was* fomenting disaffection amongst the Shi'a of southern Iraq in protest at their traditional subordination to a Sunni minority in Baghdad. (The evidence for armed Iranian incursions across the border in the same period looks, by contrast, slender. Certainly they were insignificant.) Similarly, the general belief that Khomeini's revolution was for export was at that time actively stimulated by the public utterances of the Ayatollah and his men. In Baghdad's calculations the Iranian/Shi'a threat to the cohesion of Iraq alone — quite apart from possible consequences elsewhere in the Sunni world — was reason enough for hostility, if not also for hostilities. It is difficult to reject the view that in Iraqi eyes no peace would be meaningful that did not involve Iranian assurances of 'non-interference' more binding than those written into the 1975 Algiers Agreement.[2]

If then we accept the sectarian aspect as fundamental, what importance must we attach to the purely political aspects?

Some of these can perhaps be discarded as secondary or side-issues. It seems for instance improbable that the detachment of Khuzistan[3] from Iranian sovereignty was ever a serious Iraqi war aim — although it was quite some time before there were explicit disavowals from Baghdad. It may be that the Iraqi leadership privately hoped that, as a by-product of the invasion, the Arabs in Khuzistan would welcome the Iraqis as liberators and that the transfer of the province to Iraqi sovereignty would thereby ensue as a bonus outcome of the decisive military victory they hoped for. But this was surely not a possibility inherent in Iraq's basic motivation. In public the formula more generally advanced in Iraqi statements envisaged the acquisition of autonomy for the province rather than its total severance from Iran; and so disinterested an aim could scarcely qualify as a *casus belli*.

Similarly, frontier adjustments upstream in the hinterland, however often they have figured as Iraqi *desiderata* in negotiations over the years, do not give the impression of bulking large in Baghdad's purview. (How many of us indeed have ever received a clear idea of what bits of land are involved, or why?) Further still down the line of implausibility is the periodic inclusion amongst declared Iraqi war aims of the recovery for the Arab Emirates concerned of the islands in the lower Gulf (the Tunbs and Abu Musa) seized by the Shah in 1971.[4]

But if there is doubt whether those were ever more than political side-issues, there is no doubt at all that for the Iraqis unopposed usage of the Shatt waterway and of the small stretch of Iraqi territory debouching on the Gulf is seen, in economic and security terms, as vital. It is true that Saddam Hussein's own 1975 agreement with the Shah had accepted, for the first time in the history of the dispute, shared sovereign control over the Shatt on the basis of the *thalweg*; but the vital principle of unopposed Iraqi usage of the waterway was not thereby placed at risk. What did place it (and increasingly) at risk was the subsequent threat of Shi'a revolt in the southern half of the state at Iranian instigation. The two issues — the security of the state as a cohesive unity and the security of the Shatt as Iraq's only southern channel to the outside world — were accordingly inseparable. By Iraqi standards, if not by those of international law,[5] a pre-emptive military strike at Iran was therefore justifiable. Iran's alleged disregard for some of the provisions of the 1975 Algiers Agreement and Iraq's 'consequent' denunciation of it in September 1980 were no more than symptoms of a deepening antipathy and distrust. Obviously, however, the fact that the agreement could be so easily jettisoned may prove an obstacle to a definitive peace.

This leaves, amongst the political motivations which have been advanced for the clash of arms, the wider issue of regional hegemony. No one assuredly supposes that Iranian aspirations to a dominant position in the region disappeared with the Shah; nor has the Khomeini regime done much to promote such a supposition. (For that matter, any conceivable successor regime, for reasons of national or Farsi pride, would assuredly renew pressure sooner or later for Iranian dominance in the Gulf area.) Equally there is little doubt that the development over the years of Iraqi wealth and weight, if not of Iraqi ideology, had led it (and still leads it) to aspire to local hegemony. And certainly their respective aspirations to regional influence spelt active rivalry between Saddam Hussein's Iraq and Khomeini's Iran.

The belief that these wider political ambitions and counter-ambitions were the real, if unstated, cause of the war, and that all other (stated) objectives should therefore be subsumed within it as subordinate, was and remains widespread. If the belief is correct, three observations may nonetheless be in place.

First, while Iraq may certainly have hoped to overthrow the Khomeini regime, that is a different matter from reducing a neighbour country with a population three or four times as large as Iraq's and with economic potential and technological expertise to match, to lasting powerlessness.

Secondly, regional influence in any part of the world, being the earned product of a whole series of factors, is hardly something decided in a short space of time by force of arms. Or if that is too rational a view, regional influence is at any rate not a primary aim of war in the sense of something that can be apportioned in an ensuing peace treaty, even a peace treaty imposed in the context of outright military victory.

Thirdly, even if a regional hegemony was the fundamental Iraqi objective, this was never spelt out in terms. In the event of military victory falling to Iraq, what Iraq would have to demand of a peace treaty would be the explicit fulfilment of its declared but lesser objectives, the public satisfaction of its stated grievances. In the context of peacemaking, therefore, the specific war aims we had identified as basic retain their pride of place.

To these, then, let us return. The conclusion reached so far is that, even if some of the explanations advanced for the war are unconvincing or secondary, nonetheless its basic motivations must be admitted as multiple — political, sectarian, personal. And each of the declared objectives which we have adopted as fundamental will doubtless have to be visibly remedied if peace is to be restored. Provided, that is, that the course of events has not rendered any of them obsolete. If, for example, Saddam Hussein's main initial objective was the overthrow of Khomeini, it must have ceased to be so now. The satisfaction of that particular *desideratum* can hardly be an Iraqi precondition today for an armistice. Khomeini's counter-insistence on the removal of Saddam Hussein, however, may be of a different nature: a point to which we shall return.

Let us next turn to the reasons — at any rate the ostensible reasons — why the efforts of successive mediators have so far failed to separate the combatants, measuring these against the basic causes we have identified for the outbreak of war.

Obviously, as long as the war was seen by the Iraqis as going in their favour and the cost of continuing it until Iran was suitably humbled was regarded as tolerable, efforts to persuade them to withdraw from Iranian territory fell on deaf ears — partly perhaps because they never had any clear conception of how far in geographical terms their penetration of Iran *needed* to go. By the middle of 1982 the initiative had passed to the Iranians and the situation looked like being reversed. It was consequently during the intervening period, when neither side conspicuously held the military advantage, that successful mediation must have seemed possible to many outsiders. Attempts had of course started earlier; and by mid-1981 the first crop — which the Kissinger school would no doubt describe as being undertaken before the problem was 'ripe' — had aborted. Can anything be learnt from them?

The first were the three missions carried out between November 1980 and February 1981 by Olof Palme on behalf of the UN Secretary-General. On his second visit he was told by Saddam Hussein[6] that the Iraqi armies would withdraw from Iran if the latter 'recognized Iraq's territorial rights' — although ten days earlier Saddam Hussein had been reported as declaring that Iraq refused to withdraw (and negotiate) because of the danger that Iran would thereupon invade Iraq. After his third visit Palme was reported[7] to have reached the conclusion that the two states were 'doomed to run this river jointly' — the implication being that it was this issue (control over the Shatt) which had bulked largest in his discussions and on which he had found the disputants irreconcilable.

Later the same month (February 1981) a high-level nine-man mediation committee set up by the Islamic Conference Organization visited both capitals and was reported[8] to have canvassed a formula under which Iraq would pull back after two weeks and the two sides should thereupon together submit their claims to Islamic arbitration. The committee was rebuffed — by, amongst others, Bani Sadr, whom the Iranian religious leaders were then loudly criticizing for the inadequacy of his military achievements. Perhaps for that reason he declared that he would accept nothing less favourable than the 1975 Agreement (in other words, the application to the Shatt of the *thalweg* principle), that the Iraqis must in any case withdraw from Iran before any negotiation could take place, and that the aggressors must be publicly condemned.[9]

By the time the same committee tried again in May 1981, a

mission from the Non-Aligned Movement had also made an attempt at mediation. What Saddam Hussein appears to have told this group was that he was all in favour of peace, on condition of Iraqi control of the Shatt (the condition just ruled out by Bani Sadr) and on condition also of the return of the Gulf islands seized ten years earlier by the Shah.[10] So this group too returned empty-handed — as they did from a second attempt three months later.

Although Khomeini continued before, during and after this period to demand Saddam Hussein's head on a platter it will be noticed that the common issue on which these mediation efforts ostensibly foundered was control over the Shatt. It does not necessarily follow that this was the consideration uppermost in the combatants' minds. But what perhaps did follow from the apparent insistence by both sides on the primacy of this issue was that hostilities would certainly continue until a formula for dealing with it could be discovered which each could sell to its constituents as honourable.

By autumn 1981 *The Times*, in a leader significantly entitled 'Islam's Forgotten War',[11] declared that Iraq's war aims were 'still unaltered': namely, recognition of Iraqi sovereignty over the Shatt, the transfer of bits of territory theoretically ceded to Iraq in the 1975 Agreement, and the reaffirmation of the clause in that Agreement under which each side pledged to refrain from subversive interference in the other. Nor was there any visible change in the rigidity of the Iranian stance: rather the reverse, since as the months passed Iran's military posture was improving.

Nonetheless, the mediators struggled on — both the same agencies as before (Olof Palme, the Islamic Conference Organization and the Non-Aligned Movement) and a few others, notably an Algerian initiative, which suffered a setback from the death of its leader, the Algerian Foreign Minister, in an air crash in April 1982. Published explanations of their lack of success are not uniform. But a softening of Iraqi demands, as the year proceeded and as the military advantage swung in Iran's favour, is apparent; and some verbal reshaping of Iranian conditions seemed momentarily encouraging. For in April 1982 both combatants were speaking in terms of a committee of enquiry into who started the war[12] — a proposal incorporated into the Islamic Conference Organization's four-point plan put forward towards the end of that month. The other three points it envisaged were the withdrawal of Iraqi troops, the stationing of Islamic forces on the border and the appointment of an Islamic Commission to seek a settlement of the Shatt issue.[13]

But the Iranians now demanded unconditional Iraqi withdrawal, reparations and the restoration of the 1975 Agreement. To these conditions was added, in Iran's response to the Algerian Peace Mission a month later, insistence on the repatriation to Iraq of 150,000 Shi'a expellees.[14] And when Saddam Hussein announced on 10 June 1982 a final decision to withdraw his forces from what little they still held of Iranian territory, Iran was unmoved, repeating the familiar demands (not least, 'punishment of the aggressor') and adding for good measure rights of passage through Iraq for Iranian troops on their way to the Lebanese war front.[15]

At this point we may pause to take stock. Three observations may be in place. First, it is of some interest that in reports of the failure of mediation efforts in the first six months of 1982 (as distinct from periodic *obiter dicta* by Iranian leaders), the removal of Saddam Hussein personally still does not figure as an explicit Iranian precondition. No doubt the insistence on a war-crimes tribunal and punishment of the aggressor envisaged precisely that result; but presumably the implementation of an armistice would not have to await the outcome of any such judicial procedure. Secondly, ever since Iran's military successes round Dezful in March 1982, the concern reportedly uppermost in Iraqi perspectives was the fear that Iran now aimed to transfer the fighting into Iraq, by whatever means. In a contemporary assessment by Patrick Seale,[16] it was by means of a popular Shi'a uprising in Iraq that Iran hoped to achieve the downfall of Saddam Hussein's regime. If such an uprising was ever likely, the likelihood must have been greatest when Iranian forces did indeed transfer the fighting into Iraqi territory three months later. But even then there was no sign amongst the Iraqi Shi'a of revolt or defection. If Iranian strategy was indeed predicated on a mass transfer of allegiance by them, the fact that this could now be seen as a miscalculation must have made its mark in Tehran — much as the refusal by the Khuzistan Arabs to welcome the Iraqi invaders in 1980/81 must have then affected strategic thinking in Baghdad. Thirdly, the point was being reached in the war when the Iranians for their part had successfully driven out the Iraqi invaders and the Iraqis for theirs had successfully driven back the initial Iranian counter-invasion — a point at which both sides could plausibly have claimed a victory and hostilities could have been called off without loss of face. But the chance to exploit that fleeting situation was missed.

By the end of 1982, whereas Iraq's posture had become distinctly more ready for compromise, there was still little change in Iran's — partly no doubt because the Iranians still felt they had the military edge. Conventional mediation remained unable to bridge the chasm; and less conventional manoeuvres, by the Saudi government in particular, to promote an end to the war, had made no progress either.[17]

If the Iranians continued to hope for the setting up of an Islamic Republic in at least the southern half of Iraq, it must by now have been apparent to them that the outright defeat or collapse of the Iraqi armed forces was a necessary preliminary. But to most outside observers a prolonged war of attrition was a much more likely prospect. Iraq for its part was obtaining from France (openly)[18] and from the Soviet Union (less openly)[19] a supply of sophisticated weaponry; the fact that its troops now had their backs to the wall clearly restored their fighting spirit (and most of them, let it be remembered, are Shi'a); and Iran's huge reserves of untrained manpower appeared to some observers to be at least balanced by the strength and quality of Iraqi battle-troops. There may still be plenty of teenage Iranian zealots prepared to rush into battle and die for Khomeini, but their sacrifice will not in most military calculations win a modern war.

A war of attrition is of course a gloomy enough military prospect. But so far as Iraq is concerned, the military strain seems less likely to cause a weakening of will than the financial strain. Iraq's oil exports are reduced to a mere 600,000 b/d; and by late 1982 payment by Saudi Arabia and the Gulf states of their huge regular war subventions to Iraq was evidently faltering — although the statement by the Iraqi Deputy Premier Tariq Aziz to *Le Monde* on his January 1983 visit to Paris that Iraq's 'Arab brothers have virtually stopped helping us for the last twelve months'[20] must have struck those Arab brothers as less than gracious. Possibly the warnings issuing from Tehran in autumn 1982 to the Gulf states that support for Iraq would not go unpunished by a victorious Iran caused them some alarm. Be that as it may, OPEC's decision in March 1983 both to cut oil prices by $5 per barrel and to reduce production must have put the continued receipt by Iraq of these gigantic Arab subsidies (generally estimated to have reached $25 billion by the end of 1982) seriously at risk.

No similar financial considerations appear to affect Iran. However damaging the war must be to its economy, its oil exports have shown remarkable resilience, having climbed back to 3.2 million b/d; the installations on Kharg island appear to be provided with such sophisticated defences as to be virtually impregnable; and even a major drop in price per barrel will not leave it without substantial income or impose on it the same financial strain as may overtake Iraq.

This of course does not mean that Iraq will be obliged to sue unilaterally for peace. Saddam Hussein's reported statement to US pressmen in November 1982[21] that Iraq would continue the fight until Iran respects its independence and stops interfering doubtless remains true. Its armed forces seem to be in good enough shape to ensure that Iran's will not break through to Baghdad or Basra or any other vital strategic goal; and whatever its economic plight, there is an evident unwillingness on the part of the outside world (and not only of such Arabs in it as would directly suffer) to see Iraq plunged into chaos.

But clearly we have travelled a long way from the days when Iraq could confidently insist on achieving the specific and fundamental war aims assessed at the beginning of this article — basically undisputed control of the Shatt and enforced security from Iranian subversive interference amongst its subjects. Not only was Saddam Hussein reported in January 1983[22] as having offered to fly to Tehran on a peace mission, but at the Non-Aligned Conference in New Delhi in March of the same year, the Iraqi delegates made the new conciliatory gesture of proposing the appointment of a non-aligned arbitration tribunal with a pledge to accept its decisions as binding.[23] These were clear signs of Iraq's willingness to compromise, but Iran's delegates at the conference repeated the familiar condition that the Iraqi aggressors must not be allowed to go unpunished. This by definition remains a point on which accommodation is not open to Iraq's present leadership.

We began by seeking to narrow down to fundamentals the specific initial war aims of the combatants. We then surveyed the successive reefs on which mediation has hitherto foundered. What then can be done, in the context of a continuing war of attrition, one which will not allow an outright military victory to either side and which is causing serious problems to the outside world as well, to secure for both parties adequate satisfaction on what remains of their fundamental war aims, personal, sectarian and political? What follows makes the reaonable assumption that by now Iraq would be content to forget any lesser (or indeed wider) objectives and secure the best deal on its two basic demands (security of usage of the Shatt and security from Iranian Shi'a subversion) that a neutral tribunal could hand down.

On the political issue of the Shatt, the conclusion reached long ago by Olof Palme would seem inescapable: the two states are 'doomed to run this river jointly'. Iran is not on record as demanding more than the restoration of the 1975 Algiers Agreement for shared control — and let us not forget that it was Saddam Hussein himself who negotiated it. What is therefore needed on this count may be no more than a rewording of the relevant passage, coupled with some kind of external guarantee — in short, a restatement which both sides can represent as an improvement. As for frontier adjustments inland — an Iraqi requirement outstanding from 1975 but whose fundamentality we have questioned — the best formula would seem to be a *quid pro quo*, involving Iranian agreement to a precise method and timetable for frontier adjustment, coupled with Iraqi acceptance of the repatriation of Shi'a expellees.

On the sectarian issue, there are some factors which suggest the possibility of relief. First, we have said that Iran ought surely to have concluded by now that an effective Shi'a uprising or defection in southern Iraq is not on the cards — if only since an outright military victory by Iran is beyond its grasp. Secondly, there have been renewed signs recently in Iranian communications to the Gulf states that the export of Khomeini's revolution has reverted to the back-burner.[24] Thirdly, the most recent wording of Iraq's insistence on non-interference has been distinctly less forcible than earlier. Once again then, a redrafting of the relevant passage in the 1975 Agreement, coupled perhaps with some external guarantee covering Iraqi non-interference in Khuzistan as well as Iranian non-interference in southern Iraq, would seem to be a possible way out.

This leaves the personal factor, what is left here being the continued Iranian demand for punishment of the aggressor and its implications for Saddam Hussein personally. Here the solution may lie in the intimations given by both sides in April 1982 of their willingness to have a committee of enquiry set up to establish responsibility for the war, coupled with Iraq's offer at the Non-Aligned Conference in New Delhi in March 1983 to accept as binding the decisions of a neutral tribunal. For it would seem improbable that any impartial tribunal would conclude that the responsibility for the war was one-sided. Be that as it may, here surely lies the only hope of the Iranian leaders relinquishing, *as a pre-condition* of ending the war, their demand for the removal of the Baathist government in general and of Saddam Hussein in particular.

None of these elements in a possible solution can be envisaged as negotiable without outside initiative. What agency would seem best placed to take it? Iranian misgivings about the neutrality of the UN, which is evidently regarded as jointly manipulated by the two superpowers, may rule that body out; and the two superpowers themselves, both of them anathema to Khomeini, are *a fortiori* out of the question as mediators. Other individual countries, though offers to mediate are legion, are probably ruled out too, since none disposes of sufficient influence and standing with both parties. The two agencies which have never ceased to use their good offices are of course the Non-Aligned Movement and the Islamic Conference Organization (ICO). The former, since its membership includes influential non-Islamic countries which Khomeini may therefore regard as disqualified and for some of which he has a personal distaste, would seem less well placed than the ICO to make a further attempt at solving the problem — although it might play a helpful part in promoting acceptance of a 'war crimes' tribunal composed itself of purely Islamic members, both Shi'a and Sunni. (A contributory effort by the Non-Aligned Movement may indeed be made expedient by Khomeini's frequent accusation of pro-Iraqi bias in the ICO.) None of this, of course, overlooks the necessity of much back-stage coming and going by other powers and people to set the scene. In this context, the response in particular of Syria to exhortations from one direction or another may well be important.

Is, the time 'ripe' (in the Kissinger terminology) for a major attempt at a solution? As pointed out by others in this volume, mediation can only succeed if the two parties are themselves privately willing to end the fighting. Mediation efforts have hitherto failed because those conditions did not obtain. Are they emerging now?

As far as the armed forces are concerned, it is difficult not to believe that they continue the fight not because they want to but because orders are orders. (This of course may not apply *tantum quantum* to the waves of young Iranian irregulars eager to sacrifice themselves for Khomeini's version of the faith; but in the military equation proper their relevance is marginal.) It is equally difficult not to believe that the Iraqi authorities would now be content with a cease-fire on terms (of the kind indicated) which they can represent as honourable. It is over the attitude of the religious hierarchy in Iran that the question mark on timing must hang. Do they yet recognize that outright military victory or occupation of crucial areas of Iraq is not achievable? And have they yet swallowed the evident fact that the primary allegiance of most Iraqi Shi'a is to their own country? (Even the religious hierarchy in Najaf and Karbala are rumoured to view the establishment in Iraq of an Islamic Republic on Khomeini's model without enthusiasm.) If the message has been digested, there is hope of progress. If not, the world may have to wait and the carnage continue.

Let us return to the subject of Khomeini's periodic insistence on the removal from power of Saddam Hussein. The wheel of fortune may of course bring a change of leadership in either country or both. On this the most that can be said is that rumours exist of an inclination amongst some of Iraq's Arab friends to promote the idea of a change in Iraq's leadership (not necessarily involving a change in its commitment to Baathism) as a catalyst for peace. Equally, it is frequently alleged that opposition from one direction or another to Khomeini's regime is growing to the point that a change in Iran too is only a matter of time. But speculation on either of these themes would be out of place here. We are left therefore with the hope that Khomeini's personal antipathy may be satisifed with the appointment of a 'war-responsibility' tribunal and a binding Iraqi pledge to accept the judgment it hands down — something, in effect, distinctly less than the withdrawal or overthrow of Saddam Hussein as a precondition for a cease-fire.

As for the question discussed at the outset as to whether a cease-fire or the emergence of an acceptable framework for a definitive peace must come first, it will be apparent that in the writer's own view the terms of the overall settlement of the political and sectarian issues, and the procedures for implementing them, will have to be privately established before any public commitment to pursuing them — and therefore to any substantive ceasefire — can be expected.

Whether such a consummation, however devoutly to be wished, would lead to peace in the second of its two senses — a comprehensive understanding to live and let live — is doubtless a different matter. It depends on whether the 'real' and overarching objective of the current hostilities was and remains the achievement of hegemony in the region as a whole, all other basic aims being subsumed within it. If that view is correct — and it is the view to which the writer is inclined to subscribe — then the best hope is that Iraq and Iran, having used war to secure a settlement of the minor fundamental points at issue, will use peace and the blessings that go with it to advance their respective claims to regional influence — the earned product, as already stated, of a whole series of legitimate and civilizing factors.

Notes

1. Instances are listed in A. E. H. Dessouki (ed.), *The Iran-Iraq War: Issues of Conflict and Prospects for Settlement* (Princeton University Press, Princeton, N. J., 1981), pp. 15–30.

2. The Text is set out in Tareq Y. Ismail, *Iran and Iraq: Roots of Conflict* (Syracuse University Press, Syracuse, N. Y., 1982), pp. 60–2 being those relevant.

3. The Iranian name for the province, rather than Arabistan, is used without prejudice in this essay, since it is under Iranian sovereignty.

4. This is not to deny the strength of the Iraqi government's feeling on the subject, of which the writer was made personally aware in December 1971.

5. See Richard Falk's analysis of this aspect in Dessouki, *The Iran-Iraq War*, pp. 79–90.

6. *New York Times*, 16 Jan. 1981.

7. Ibid., 27 Jan. 1981.

8. Agence France Presse report of 3 March 1982.

9. Reuter's report of 3 March 1981.

10. Ibid., 12 May 1981.

11. *The Times*, 21 Sept. 1981.

12. *Daily Telegraph*, 14 Apr. 1982.

13. *Egyptian Gazette*, 29 Apr. 1982.

14. *Observer*, 30 May 1982.

15. *Guardian*, 21 June 1982.

16. *Observer News Service*, 5 Apr. 1982.

17. See for instance G. H. Jansen in *Middle East International (MEI)* (4 Feb. 1983), pp. 6 & 7.

18. *Sunday Times*, 6 Feb. 1983.

19. *Contemporary Middle East Backgrounder* (an Israeli periodical) (17 Oct. 1982).

20. *Le Monde*, 8 Jan. 1983.

21. *Guardian*, 17 Nov. 1982.

22. *Daily Telegraph*, 2 Jan. 1983.

23. *MEI* (18 Mar. 1983), p. 7.

24. See for instance Michael Jansen in MEI (18 Feb. 1983), p. 8.

CONTRIBUTORS

John Duke Anthony is a former Associate Professor at Johns Hopkins University and is currently the President of the National Council on US-Arab Relations, Washington.

Glen Balfour-Paul is a Research Fellow at the Centre for Arab Gulf Studies at the University of Exeter.

Basil al-Bustany is a Professor of Economics at the University of Baghdad.

M. S. El Azhary is Deputy Director, Centre for Arab Gulf Studies at the University of Exeter.

Peter Hünseler is a Research Fellow at the Research Institute of the German Society for Foreign Affairs, Bonn.

G. H. Jansen is a journalist and writer on Middle East Affairs.

David E. Long is a senior analyst at the US Department of State.

Mustafa al-Najjar is Director of the Centre for Arab Gulf Studies at the University of Basra.

Najdat Fathi Safwat is an Iraqi Diplomat and Historian.

John Townsend is a former Economic Adviser to the Sultanate of Oman, and currently works for Business International, Geneva.

INDEX

border agreements: Algiers
Agreement, 1975 2, 19, 83, 122,
128, 129, 131, 132, 133, 136;
Constantinople Protocol, 1913
12–13, 14, 15, 19, Erzerum,
Second Treaty of, 1847 11–12, 33,
Iranian-Iraqi border treaty, 1937
15, 16, 18, Peace Treaty, 1639 10,
11, 36n65; border clashes, 1957 17;
border commissions 11, 12, 13, 15;
thalweg line principle 15, 16, 19,
129, 131
Shi'a: in Arab Gulf States 9, 86, 108,
110, 114; in Iraq 1, 9, 82, 85, 92,
128, 138; in Syria 84
Shi'ism 8, 9, 81
South Korea 125
South Yemen 85, 106
Soviet Union: arms trade 18–19, 91,
95, 101, 103n22; Middle East
policy 17, 96–102, 108, 109, 110,
111, 119–20; naval presence in
Arabian Sea 97; relations with Iran
46, 98–100, 109, Iraq 18, 19, 85,
91, 94, 97–8, 100–2, 111, Syria
97, United States of America 97,
99, Yemen People's Democratic
Republic 85, 108; *see also* Russia
Steadfastness and Confrontation
Front 4, 84, 85
Sunni-Shi'a antagonism 9, 81, 105,
113, 127, 128, 138; and Arab Gulf
States 106, 107, 108, 113–16

Syria 95, 110; relations with Iran
48, 84, 106, Iraq 48, 49, 84, 109,
117, Soviet Union 97, 111

Tariq Aziz, Iraqi deputy prime
minister 101, 134
Thamir bin Ghadhban, Ka'bid ruler
31, 32
Tudeh party 100, 110
Tunbs Islands 2, 86, 106, 129, 132
Tunisia 85, 86
Turkey 109, 117; *see also* Ottoman
Empire

United Arab Emirates 55, 106, 107,
108, 110, 113, 129
United Nations 94, 131, 137
United States of America: arms
trade with Iran 92, 93–4, 95;
Middle East policy 18, 88–96,
121–2, 124; military assistance to
Saudi Arabia 89–90, 91, 93, 97;
naval presence in Arabian Sea
89–90, 97, 102n2; relations with
Iran 17, 18, 93–4, 95, 96, 122,
Iraq 94, 111, 122, 124, Israel 121,
124

Vinogradov, Vladimir, Soviet
ambassador 99

Yemen People's Democratic Republic
85, 106